The Benefit of Using an Attorney-REALTOR®

Seven Ways to Get Moving
Fast and Safe

Hope Ries

Copyright © 2016 by Hope Ries

All rights are reserved. No part of this publication may be reproduced, stored in a retrieval system, or transmitted in any form, or by any means, electronic, mechanical, photocopying, recording, or otherwise – except for brief quotations in printed reviews – without the permission of the publisher, or Hope Ries, in writing. Nothing in this book is to be construed as legal advice.

ISBN: 978-1-77277-087-2

Published by
10-10-10 Publishing
Markham, Ontario
CANADA

Contents

Foreword	v
Acknowledgements	vii
Dedication	ix
Testimonials	xi
Chapter 1: Why You Want an Attorney-REALTOR® and Why You Need Me!	1
Chapter 2: You and Your Feelings Matter to Me	9
Chapter 3: A REALTOR® Who is Also an Excellent Communicator	35
Chapter 4: What You Say Without Speaking a Word	61
Chapter 5: Everything In Life Is Negotiable	77
Chapter 6: A REALTOR® Who Will Fight for Your Rights	95
Chapter 7: Eye on the Prize	105
Chapter 8: Bright Futures – Let's Do This Together	121
Chapter 9: Legally Speaking	131
Chapter 10: Who is Hope?	141
About the Author	150

Foreword

I had the pleasure of meeting Hope Ries at a Real Estate Event in Atlanta, Georgia. I was blown away by the transferable skills that she cultivated in her legal career, and now implements as a REALTOR®. The combination of an Attorney-REALTOR® is the safest way to be represented when buying or selling a home. I am impressed with Hope's tenacity, skill, and expertise in the Real Estate market.

The Real Estate market can change quickly and having an expert like Hope on your side is an invaluable resource and amazing advantage. Looking to buy or sell property in Georgia? Hope is the best person to represent you.

I am so amazed with Hope's level of expertise that I have asked her to contribute to my book series, *The Authorities*, a collection of Authorities in their areas of expertise, where Hope will be featured as the Real Estate authority.

In this book, *The Benefit of Using an Attorney-REALTOR®*, Hope explores all of the skills that she possesses which make her unique and stand out above other REALTORS® and agents.

When you meet Hope, you will know she is special. She has the ability to instantly connect with you, as you will see when you begin reading this book. I believe there is nothing that Hope cannot accomplish and I have all the faith in the world in Hope. I know you will enjoy this book, and it is my honor and pleasure to endorse Hope.

Raymond Aaron
New York Times Best Selling Author

Acknowledgements

So many people have helped me in my journey. I want to thank my family for being there every step of the way and never giving up on me. Brett, thanks for the love and patience. Harper and Callyn, thanks for all the laughter. Thanks to my brother, Robert, for always encouraging me and supporting me in every adventure I undertook. Mom, Dad, Laura, and Walt thanks for all the guidance and wisdom. Olivia and Ellie, I love how our relationship has blossomed into a special bond that I don't have with anyone else.

Emmy, I would not have made it through 8th grade without you; I love you. Sarah, E-liz, Bek, and Christi, thanks for being the best friends a girl could ever ask for. Your forgiveness and understanding means the world to me. I am always here if you need anything. To Delta Gamma Sorority, thank you for making me the woman I am today.

Mike Bagley, thanks for taking a chance on a recent college graduate with no experience. I appreciate your friendship and leadership, and will never forget you gave me a chance which led to all my success. Mark Gannon and Gregg Porter, thanks for mentoring and teaching me so much over the years.

To my amazing broker, and friend, DeAnn Golden, you always believed in me and instilled confidence that I could be wildly successful in real estate. I feel blessed that we met and I love working with you every day. To Rick Swan, co-broker and training extraordinaire, you always think outside the box, and provide the best nuggets of wisdom! Tanya, #marketingqueen, thank you for always making me look so good!

To all of my past and current clients, thanks for choosing me. I enjoy working with each and every one of you. It is my honor to call you a friend. I know the process of buying and selling a home can be arduous, but I hope I made the process less stressful and more fun. You know you can always call me if you need anything. I am here for you guys and I always be here.

Dedication

I dedicate this book to my sweet and loving husband, Brett, and my beautiful girls, Harper and Callyn. I love you guys so much. Thanks for sticking by me through thick and thin. We continue to keep our walls strong. I love you! Your love and support keeps me going. I am excited about our future chapters.

xoxo

Testimonials - *Zillow* reviews

1. Hope is an absolutely amazing agent. She is thorough in her home research. She gets a real feel for what you are looking for and then finds it! She knew just how to make the deal happen so we could have the home of our dreams. She is kind, compassionate and understanding. She is the kind of agent that everyone deserves!
   – Bill and Shannon, Happy clients

2. Hope has gone the extra mile to help us in many aspects. She helped us understand our options as both buyers and sellers throughout our journey. She was patient with our decisions and never pressured us to make decisions out of our comfort zone. She followed up with all agents that came to look at our house, and helped us understand their feedback. She helped us line up contractors when we had issues to repair, and helped us prioritize repairs based on a budget. She answered numerous legal questions that we had about the contract and the binding process. Her legal background made us feel secure when navigating the entire process
   – Tyler and Carly, Successful clients

Chapter 1

Why You Want an Attorney- REALTOR®, and Why You Need Me!

All REALTORS® are not created equally, and you want a REALTOR® working for you who has the acumen, skill and knowledge to ensure you get moving fast and safe. By having an attorney on your side in the real estate process, you will get my legal expertise during the entire process. In chapter 9, I will go into my childhood and how I got to where I am today; chapter 8 will fill you in on my lawyer days. After reading this book, you will have a clear understanding of why you should have an Attorney- REALTOR® on your side.

An attorney has a certain set of skills that most people do not have. I have been trained to think a certain way, act a certain way, and be highly perceptive. Not everyone has this type of education, and law school is not for everyone. I worked in the law firm environment for 15 years, and I learned things that most do not know. There are countless benefits to using me as your REALTOR®. I am a licensed and trained attorney and I will also serve as your realtor. In this book, we will explore the following reasons why I am the best realtor for you:

- I have a strong work ethic
- I am a highly effective communicator
- I am the master of contracts
- I am an internationally trained negotiator
- Everyone matters to me and I have a strong desire to help others
- I am well organized and have the ability to multi-task like no other
- I have better interpersonal skills than any other REALTOR®
- I am client-centered and goal driven
- I have an eye for detail
- I have a strong moral compass and strong ethical judgement
- I am comfortable and work confidently in high pressure situations
- I have first-rate collaboration skills
- I am never afraid to ask
- I genuinely care about my community
- I have an extensive record of success

Some of these things may seem simple to you, but do not be fooled. The average person, and certainly most REALTORS® and real estate agents, do not possess these qualities, skills or talents. Let's start with the basics. What is the difference between a real estate agent and a REALTOR®? I am a REALTOR®. This means I am a member of the NATIONAL ASSOCIATION of REALTORS®, and I am required to uphold the standards of that association as well as subscribe to a strict code of ethics. A real estate agent is anyone who takes and passes the real estate test. There are no standards for real estate agents. There are few requirements for taking the real estate test. In fact there are only six requirements in Georgia:

1. Be at least 18 years old.
2. Be a resident of the State of Georgia, unless seeking a nonresident license.
3. Pass a state real estate examination.
4. Be a high school graduate or holder of a certification of equivalency.
5. Obtain a criminal history report from the GBI (Georgia Bureau of Investigation).
6. Complete a 75 hour salesperson pre-license course, attending all the sessions.

There is no limit to the number of times a person can take the real estate test, and only 61% of people pass on their first time taking the test. There is no formal class required to take the test. You can do a self-study, in home, or on-line class before taking the test. Obviously, things are learned in the class or self-study, but the majority of agents are far from experts on contracts or any other aspects in the real estate field. I have had many people tell me they took the test multiple times before passing. Frankly, the test was not that difficult, and if a person had to take the test four times before passing, and had that much trouble passing the test, you probably do not want them negotiating one of the biggest purchases you will ever make in your life.

The next question is, probably: What are the standards of the NATIONAL ASSOCIATION of REALTORS®? Good question. There is a Code of Ethics and Standards of Practice of the NATIONAL ASSOCIATION of REALTORS® that set duties we have to our clients and customers, to the public, and to other REALTORS®. The preamble states that REALTORS® "continuously strive to become and remain informed on issues affecting real estate." Other important aspects include punishment for "misappropriation of client or customer funds or property, willful discrimination, or fraud resulting in substantial economic harm." You want someone who agrees to NOT steal your money. Why would you use someone who does not make that promise? You want someone like myself to be handling your funds so that you know you are SAFE and your money is SAFE. I am someone you can trust. Not only am I a REALTOR®, but I am also a licensed attorney who has sworn to uphold the Georgia Rules of Professional Conduct. This binds me to a strict code of ethics that I bring with me into my Real Estate career.

Article 1, of The Code of Ethics and Standards, goes into my duties as a REALTOR®, to you, my client. We are obligated to treat all parties honestly in a transaction. We are not allowed to mislead or induce the buyers, sellers, or tenants. REALTORS® are also bound to keep clients information confidential, and not use the information to the disadvantage of the client, or to the advantage of third parties, unless they consent to it. As a REALTOR®, I also have duties to the public, including giving equal representation to all people regardless of race, color, religion, sex, handicap, familial status, national origin, sexual orientation, or gender identity.

Along those same lines, when involved in the sale or lease of a residence, REALTORS® shall not volunteer information regarding the racial, religious, or ethnic composition of any neighborhood. When **NOT** involved in the sale or lease of a residence, REALTORS® may provide demographic information related to a property if the information is (a) deemed by the REALTOR® to be necessary in order to assist with, or complete a real estate transaction or professional assignment, and (b) is obtained or derived from a recognized, reliable, independent, and impartial source. Honesty is of the utmost importance to me when representing you as your REALTOR®.

Finally, we owe a duty to other REALTORS® to not knowingly or recklessly make false or misleading statements about other real estate professionals, their businesses, or their business practices. This is where REALTORS® duties end. But a mere real estate agent is not bound by any standards or code of ethics which will be detrimental to you, regardless of what side of the transaction you are on, be it buyer or seller.

In this book, *The Benefits of Using an Attorney Realtor,* you will be let in on the many reasons why I am the best available resource for anyone looking to list a home for sale or buy a home, or are an investor looking to buy many properties. There are no other REALTORS® that can offer the same skills and experience that will provide the sense of security that I offer my clients. As you read my book, I will refer back to my legal career and the lessons I learned in the 15 years I worked in a law firm environment. I will not shy away from my background and the lessons I learned in the courtroom and my law practice. I am very transparent on why things are important – my legal career and how it translates into my real estate career, and why this is invaluable to you as my real estate client.

My work ethic cannot be matched by anyone in the legal field or real estate field. You either have a strong work ethic or you don't. Once a person reaches a certain age, they either have a strong work ethic or they do not; it is not something you can teach. I began working from a young age and I have never stopped working. Growing up, we lived very frugally and had a very tight purse. We had to be creative about ways to earn money. Without a doubt, this instilled in me a work ethic like no other. I always give 110% at every job I ever work at. As your REALTOR®, you will get my 110%. My Type A personality likely plays a role in my strong work ethic.

My strong work ethic can be a double edged sword, leading to working long hours and wanting perfection. In my legal career, I worked more hours than any other attorney in the office. I would get to the office before anyone else and would leave after everyone else. This is partly what made me such a successful attorney. My work ethic made me always want to get things completed. A strong work ethic is not something that can be turned on and off at will. As a person who came from meager beginnings, I learned from a young age the importance and value of money, which helped instill a strong work ethic. Moreover, I think by seeing that hard work pays off, it pushed me to keep working hard. Seeing results from my hard work helped me keep moving forward. My strong work ethic has helped me find success in all aspects of my life because I will never give up. I strive for success and have a client-centered attitude. I want to help others, and the service of others feeds my soul.

As your REALTOR®, I have an interest in you, and to help you. I went to law school and became an attorney so I could help others. That was the main reason for me going to law school. I knew I would be able to help others. I love that part of real estate. I like to be able to help people see their way through situations. I get to help people in a time of need, which is an honor. I will discuss in detail my background and childhood so you'll know where I came from. I think this is very important for you as my reader to have an understanding of who I am and why I am the way I am. I rose to the top of my legal profession, which I will also outline for you – not to be braggadocios, but so you know I am the real deal. Finally, I will provide you with the reasons I decided to make my career change from law to real estate.

My reasons for leaving the law, and transitioning into Real Estate, will give you a perspective on what makes me the right REALTOR® for you. The decision to change careers after 15 years of working exclusively in the legal profession was one I took very seriously; however, I could not be happier with my change. It is my honor and pleasure to be working in the real estate business and to be a member of Berkshire Hathaway HomeServices. I joined the best real estate firm in the country, if not the world. I am proud to be associated with Berkshire Hathaway, and I wear their name proudly. For details on the services I offer, visit my website at www.hoperiesattorneyrealtor.com.

Chapter 2

You and Your Feelings Matter to Me

As your REALTOR®, I will never take for granted that your feelings, your voice, and your opinion are integral parts of the process. Many of you read that sentence, thinking, "No joke, it is all about me." You are correct, but many people who work in the real estate business make it about themselves and lose sight of their clients in the process.

In my law practice, I was always dealing with people's personal lives and matters that were delicate and often painful, but it was my job to discuss these matters in detail and at length. This part of my law practice, difficult as it was, gives me such an advantage in my real estate career. It is crucial to be able to make people feel comfortable so they are willing to open up to you, but making them comfortable enough to open up can prove difficult. The more comfortable a person is around you, the more they will open up, and you can get to the heart of what matters to them. In real estate, as your REALTOR®, I am looking for the true purpose of your move.

People will say things like, "We need a bigger house," or "Our house is too small," or "We want a bigger yard," or "We want to live in the city," or "We want a new house." All of these answers are fine and appropriate responses to the question of why you are moving, but they do not really get to the true purpose of the move. The true purpose may be that they are moving to a bigger house because they are expecting a child, or they are downsizing because they are empty nesters. They may be moving because of a new job offer, or need a smaller home due to loss of a job. There are many different reasons that are the true purpose of the move. People tend to give an initial superficial response as to why they are moving, and not the true purpose. As your REALTOR®, I want to know the purpose behind the move because it will provide me with significant information that is useful to me.

So many of my skills that I perfected as an attorney, make me an incredibly effective REALTOR®. Many attorneys see themselves as being better than others, and can be very arrogant; REALTORS® are not so different. I was not that type of attorney, and never thought of myself as better than anyone. I have always tried to live my life by the motto of *treating people the way I would want to be treated.* The golden rule, "So whatever you wish that others would do to you, do also to them…" No matter what the person's situation in life, they should be treated with respect and kindness. People can have a rough exterior that can quickly dissolve with a hint of kindness.

I always treat people the way I would want to be treated, or how I would want my mother, grandmother, or any other family member to be treated. I think this is one of life's most valuable lessons. In my law practice, I dealt with a myriad of different people – people who didn't speak English, middle class people, highly uneducated people, as well as doctors, lawyers, and judges. Regardless of their station in life or their background, I spoke to them respectfully and with kindness. Even if we were on opposing sides, I was respectful. Time and time again I would see other attorneys speak down to people, talk over them, or intentionally use language the person did not understand. Sometimes it was obvious the attorney was doing this to frustrate a witness, or make them feel stupid, or to show their own superiority. I never found this to be an effective technique, and people never responded well to this tactic. This doesn't make people open up or want to provide you more information; they usually get angry, frustrated or shut down completely.

There is one event in my law career that stands out to me, and I have taken it with me. I will never treat any person or client the way this person was treating another person. In my area of practice, attorneys would often take or steal cases from other attorneys. I tried to avoid taking cases from other attorneys. I never wanted the reputation of being the type of attorney who would steal a case, and I liked to work my cases up the way I wanted to from start to finish. There were a few occasions I felt like I had no choice, and this story involves one of those times.

On this occasion, I had a potential client come to me, begging me to take their case. She described herself as desperate and said she was not getting anywhere with her current representation. She told me that her current attorney told her that she was uneducated, didn't know anything about the law, and just needed to let him do his job. She said he talked down to her and made her feel like "mud on the bottom of his shoes." She was very upset while she was telling me this. The woman had worked very hard her entire life, had a good heart, and needed someone to help her. The attorney had been representing her for a significant amount of time, but had not done anything to move her case forward, and, at one point, tried to get her to accept a nominal settlement to "get rid of her."

Sadly, she trusted the attorney and thought he had her best interest in mind. She thought, since he was an attorney, he knew what he was doing and that it was alright for him to treat her the way he did. She also believed that he would help her; however, it got to the point that he was trying to convince her to do something she was not comfortable doing, and did not want to do. The attorney spoke to her this way for over a year and would never answer any questions that she asked. The poor woman was always shot down and was eventually told that she had to do something to the attorney, or her case would be over. I'm not sure how, but finally she came to me. I am very glad she did, so that s she could receive the representation she deserved.

After hearing this woman's story of how this attorney treated her, there was no way I was not going to help her. The attorney who was representing her had been practicing for a long time, and I came to learn the attorney spoke to all of the clients in that manner. I represented this client for a number of years and took her case to trial, and received a very positive outcome/verdict. To think the former attorney wanted her to go away and accept a nominal amount of money to end her case, that attorney didn't deserve to represent this client, and didn't deserve to practice law.

It is sad that the client had such a negative experience and dealt with an attorney who showed her no respect and spoke down to her. All she wanted was someone to help her. As a client, she was never pushy or rude, or tried to tell me what to do, and she always did everything I asked of her. I wish all of my clients were like her. She was always very grateful and appreciative and referred me so many other cases. This is an excellent example of how some attorneys think it is okay to speak to people in a certain manner and not treat others with respect; however, I am sure if anyone were to treat that attorney, his wife, mother, or child in the way he treated his own clients, he would have been highly offended. Again, not all attorneys are like this one and plenty of attorneys treat their clients with respect and dignity. As a REALTOR®, I have continued living by the Golden Rule and treat people the way I want to be treated. I do this across the board with clients, other agents, and anyone and everyone involved in a transaction.

You cannot practice law or real estate in a bubble; you have to work with other people and will often work with the same people repeatedly. People enjoy working with me and enjoy being on the other side of a transaction with me. This is a huge benefit to you as my client. In my law practice, I worked with the same attorneys and other people over and over, which I liked. There were some attorneys whose names I would see and I knew that we would get along, and others names I would see and know that it would be difficult to get anything accomplished.

I had the reputation of being straightforward, honest, easy to deal with it, and ethical. I wanted my reputation to proceed me, and all attorneys at any law firms knew I would treat them with respect and kindness. I never swore at other attorneys or made personal attacks, regardless of what they said to me, or their position in a case. There is no place for personal attacks in the practice of law or real estate. As your REALTOR®, you will know that the agent on the other side will have a positive experience working with me, which can make a significant difference. In a multiple offer situation, if one of the agents is nasty, a jerk, or unpleasant without a doubt, I have a leg up on that agent. I have been told by agents in multiple offer situations that they have decided on my buyer's bid, partly because I was the agent, and they knew dealing with me would be easy. This is a significant benefit to you.

Don't get me wrong. There are times when tough love is necessary, and a message needs to be delivered in a more forceful manner in order to get your point across, or to impart the seriousness of the situation. That does not mean that you should speak to somebody like they are stupid or incompetent. You can change your tone and demeanor to make sure you get the message across to them. We will discuss this more in the next chapter. There is never an excuse or need to bully a client. You want your REALTOR® to be friendly and nice to you and others, and live by the Golden Rule, as I do.

Often, in real estate and in law, people tend to treat people differently based on how long they think they have been practicing law or working on real estate. They treat older agents or attorneys with more respect, and will try and talk over people they think are younger or less experienced. This always makes me nuts, and is insanely rude and disrespectful. Clearly, this is in violation of the Golden Rule. I will never behave that way, so you will receive the benefits of my behavior.

In the last few years of my law practice, I was on top of my game and had the highest production of anyone in my department in the firm. I was a partner and had been appointed by the chief judge to serve on an ethics committee, at the judge's leisure. I spoke at various continuing legal education seminars, and other legal events and symposiums. I mentored younger attorneys, and had the respect of my peers. I was an expert in my practice areas, and my clients were lucky to have me representing them. I took genuine interest in each person, case, and the outcome of the case. This is part of what made me such an excellent attorney. I took a personal interest and I cared about my clients. I lived every day of my practice by the golden rule. If I ever needed an attorney to represent me, I would want an attorney like myself handling my case. My real estate career is no different. I take an interest in every client, and care where they end up – literally – in regard to what home they select.

I have had clients who have loved houses that had so many problems and issues, but for whatever reason, they could not see past some of these glaring problems. They really think that the home is the right home for them, and they want to love it there – they can fix the massive water stain in the foyer where they walk in; they are not worried about the deck that is about to fall off out back, and the fact that they could very likely face a significant lawsuit and lose the home if anyone is on, or under, the deck when that happens. When such things happen, I always ask myself, "What would I want someone to do if the roles were reversed, and I was about to make an ill-advised decision?" Without a doubt, I would want someone to shoot me straight and tell me what I am not seeing, and not let me buy the house. As your REALTOR®, I feel this is my duty.

Just recently, I had a couple who was looking at a house, and they were in love with the home, the neighborhood, and the perfect schools; it was everything they wanted and the price was incredible. They went to look at the home at an open house, and the agent at the open house practically begged them to make an offer; "ANY offer," were the exact words (imagine if that were your REALTOR®). My clients called me and were telling me about this perfect house they had found and about the agent's statement about making an offer. I set up an appointment to go and see the house myself.

As I pulled in the driveway, I immediately began noticing significant issues that caused significant fear for my buyers. I wrote down two pages of things that were wrong with the home, and not little minor things like dings in the wall. Not only were there some significant structural issues, there were other issues that would cost in excess of $100,000.00. There were several areas of the home in which I noticed were areas that would expose the buyers to potential lawsuits from a liability standpoint. There is no other REALTOR® who can provide you with advice regarding the potential of liabilities and lawsuits a home may contain, which can cost you your home after you purchase. One lawsuit can wipe a person out, causing them to lose more than just their home. Noticing these potential liabilities is in my DNA. Having a REALTOR® capable of doing this for you will keep you very safe in the home buying process, and for years to come. With my clients, I found their interaction with the other agent interesting on several levels.

When they inquired about issues with the house – specific issues – the agent failed to disclose the problems. She was honest about some things, but not others. She also begged for an offer on her own, which is frankly embarrassing. The agent was representing the seller of the home, and was gravelling with a potential buyer for an offer – any offer. She was essentially telling my clients that the seller was desperate and would take less then list price. This was a clear violation of the duties a REALTOR® owes to a client. The person may have been an agent; therefore, they may not have been bound by any duty. Finally, she failed to ask my clients if they were working with a

REALTOR®, which should always be asked. Take this as a warning reader – that could be who is representing you! You need me!

I believe that all people in the process, matter. From the person who answers the phone or opens the door, all the way up to the CEO of the company. Each person serves a function and plays an important role in the process. In treating each person well, I get the most that each person has to offer. As my client, you will get the benefit of my kindness to others. In real estate I am my own boss and own my own business. I am responsible for myself; however, I am blessed and fortunate to work for Berkshire Hathaway HomeServices, which is a brokerage that believes in instilling value in every REALTOR®, and they believe that every REALTOR® in the company matters.

There is no competition between agents, and we all treat each other with respect. Everyone in the brokerage collaborates, and, to some degree, works together as a team. There is no fear of sharing information and positive experiences with various vendors. There is a strong sense of family at Berkshire; we value each other and help one another. There is no competition or stealing of clients within my brokerage. If another REALTOR® is in need of help, someone will typically step up and offer to help. When I can, I try and be available to anyone who needs help, so if I need help in the future, they will return the favor.

When I am your REALTOR®, you get the full power and backing of Berkshire Hathaway HomeServices. Visit my website www.hoperiesattorneyrealtor.com for more information on Berkshire Hathaway.

When I first got into real estate, I interviewed several brokerages, and I had friends who worked in real estate with other brokerages. I heard horror stories about the real estate business being dog eat dog, which didn't scare me, coming from a legal background. My thought was that it could not be worse than the competitive practice of law and how other attorneys treated one another, and the interoffice competition. It's funny to look back and think of the things that people told me were the pitfalls and downfalls of real estate, because, in fact, they had nothing on the practice of law. I like a laid back environment, and I needed a brokerage that would suit me.

I took interviewing brokerages very seriously, and I noticed a distinct difference when I interviewed Berkshire Hathaway HomeServices and met my brokers. It wasn't all about numbers and money, but about how to be successful, how to last in the business, and the importance in investing in me and the importance of teamwork. I didn't just hear it from my broker, but I saw it in action in the office when I was there. At Berkshire Hathaway, the broker acknowledged the benefits of having an attorney-REALTOR®, and what an amazing combination it was.

She knew that I had so much to offer buyers, sellers and investors, and would be wildly successful. When I visited other brokerages, there was a lot of *rah-rah* and over the top talking, but I did not see it in action in the brokerage. I certainly took note of that. There was a different attitude. All the brokerages realized what an asset I would be for them, but it was an easy decision to make. I found a brokerage to call home, and Berkshire Hathaway has been just that. I love that there is no competition within the brokerage.

All brokerages do not operate this way and many are competitive amongst themselves, similar to a law firm atmosphere. I did not want to be part of an organization that had inter-organization competition. I chose to work at law firms that didn't have that atmosphere; and I certainly did not want that in my real estate career so that you, my clients, would never feel anything but secure with me and the brokerage I was associated with. From the CEO of Berkshire Hathaway HomeServices, Georgia Properties, Dan Forsman, to the person who answers the phone at my brokerage, everyone is willing to help each other. In fact, the CEO, Dan Forsman, has been named the most admired CEO for the last two years, and is in the running in 2016, but the winners have yet to be announced.

This is not surprising to anyone who knows him. He is incredibly involved in the company and always takes time to speak with people. He comes to company functions, looks you in the eye, shakes your hand and gives you common sense advice. He is actively driving the ship in a positive direction. The same holds true for the two brokers at my office who are always present and available for me so that you get exactly what you need. I also collaborate with the other REALTORS® out of my office. We all have our individual businesses and operate them the way we choose, but we also work together and collaborate as a team to better serve our clients. This collaboration is key and gives you, my client, and a wealth of knowledge.

One of the most amazing things about Berkshire Hathaway is the established Mentor Program where young/new agents have the chance to be paired with agents who have been in the business for a long time, and collaborate with them in an effort to get them to succeed quicker. Why keep success in a box? The company believes in sharing knowledge, which is amazing. With me as your REALTOR®, you will gain the knowledge of all the agents in my office as well. When I thought about leaving my legal career, I was excited to be my own boss, but I didn't realize that I would still have the opportunity to work in a team environment that collaborated. I am glad to still have that.

I love working with others and collaborating in an effort to get something accomplished. As long as you are in any career, there is always something new that will come your way. As a REALTOR®, there is never a dull moment and always a new adventure. A buyer will fall in love with a house that has an issue you have not dealt with before. I have my network of REALTORS® and a significant database of every other type of vendor so that you, my client, have access to whatever you need, when you need it. Sellers can have the same issues that will arise in the home they are trying to sell. Having been an attorney has put me in contact with so many different types of people that my network and resources are vast. It is a huge benefit to my clients that I seem to always know a guy or gal who can help in whatever random situation we find ourselves and need help with. Even though I meet many of these resources in my law practice, I continue to collaborate and work with them in real estate.

I also love collaborating with buyers and sellers as well. When a seller is selling their home, they have an end goal in mind of finding a buyer who wants their home within a certain amount of time. Sometime they are moving and need to find a new home, or they may be building a new home. There can be many different time lines. In order to make a deal go through, the seller's agent and the buyer's agent must collaborate and work together towards the mutual goal of the seller and the buyer. The process can be so much more enjoyable when working with an agent that is easy to work with, and there is mutual respect for one another. Having a REALTOR® like me makes the collaboration process significantly easier, no matter what side of the transaction I am on.

Most home sellers are emotionally attached to the home they are selling. This is completely normal. Typically, they have lived in the home for a number of years and have made memories and shared special moments that they will never forget. They are used to seeing their home in a certain way, which is the way they live in the home with their personal effects surrounding them. Homes are set up to be comfortable, convenient, and what works best for the home owners. Most homes are not set up to show and sell. Where you have your couch placed to watch TV in the evening may not be the best placement when you are trying to sell your home.

Often, things may need to be slightly re-arranged and you have to think of things from a potential buyer's perspective. As your REALTOR®, it is my job to tell you these things, and be honest with you about the things that need to be re-arranged, and I do not mind telling you the reason why. The biggest issue with homes when they are being sold is the need to get stuff out of the home, because it is hard to see clutter when you are living in it. Virtually everyone can live with less stuff in their home, and people need to declutter and take things out of the home in order to sell it.

The Benefit of Using an Attorney-REALTOR®

As a seller's REALTOR®, I will collaborate with you to explain why it is important to move the couch somewhere else, depersonalize the house, or think about getting a new towel and not using them. The white towels that they got ten years ago when they got married are not as white as they used to be; and, sure, the pictures of their kids are absolutely adorable, and I love their children, but a potential buyer doesn't necessarily care. Things that are special to the seller are not necessarily important to whoever is walking through the door. In fact, it may not even be a family or someone who will live in the home; it may be an investor. As a REALTOR®, it is important to try and help take the emotion out of things for sellers. I do understand how personal the home selling process is for people, and I do my best to try and take the emotion out of it for the sellers, and allow them to see it from the potential buyer's eyes. For tips on staging your home to sell, visit my website at www.hoperiesattorneyrealtor.com.

For me, it is the opposite when you're working with buyers. I always want to see a buyer have an emotional reaction or attachment to a home, which signals they have potentially found the right home. I relate finding a home to finding the right wedding dress. You know when you find the right one. I felt that way when I tried on my wedding dress. I'm sure that any woman who has gotten married and tried on wedding dresses can relate. You try on a million different dresses of all shapes and sizes, but when you try on THE dress, you know it. I'll never forget that moment. I was with my two best friends, Sarah and Christi. We were in the bridal shop, having so much fun, laughing, trying on dresses, and being silly; but, the second I put on THE dress, all three of us were speechless, and tears came to my eyes. Both Sarah and Christi also became emotional, and all three of us knew. I knew it was THE dress. Visit my website at www.hoperiesattorneyrealtor.com to see me in my wedding dress.

As your REALTOR®, when we are out looking at homes, I am looking for you to have an emotional connection to a home. When you find a home that fits the buyer, and you see them start to emotionally put themselves in the home, you know they are on the right track. Buyers get an emotional feeling about a home when they start to think it is the right one. When a buyer starts talking about where their furniture would go, how much the kids would like the yard, how great the flow is for their annual Thanksgiving dinner, the emotion comes into play.

When I bring buyers back for a second showing, you can see the emotions growing stronger, or when the buyers want to bring a friend or loved one to see the home they are considering, that is always an emotional sign. As a REALTOR®, I love this part of my job, it's a happy, warm and fuzzy feeling. I like providing this feeling to others. In order to buy a home, the buyers need to have an emotional attachment to the home and be able to see themselves in the home. When they bring in the family who praise their decision, you can see the buyer's relief. Without the emotional feeling, an offer will not be made on a home. This is human nature.

Sometimes buyers will start to second-guess their choice of a home, and, as their REALTOR®, I like to take them to other homes to see how they feel. I'll ask them, "How do you feel in this home? Do you get the same feeling in this home that you get in the other home?" I also ask the same question about the neighborhood. Nine times out of ten, they don't have the same emotional connection to the other homes that they have to the first home they found, but they just needed to be reminded of the emotion they felt in the home. It can be such a long time between going into the home and making an offer, getting through due diligence, and making it to closing. I think this emotion and feeling is very important when buying a house. Maybe I should coin this phrase the *wedding dress feeling.* When it fits, it just fits. The right house will fit, and the buyer will know it when they are in the home. I guess men can't relate to my wedding dress analogy unless they wore a dress to their wedding! Maybe men have that feeling when they meet their future bride.

Buyers will also have distinct emotional reactions to homes in a negative way as well. If certain aspects of a home remind them of a painful time in their life, or an unpleasant memory, there will be an immediate emotional reaction. As their REALTOR®, I take note of this and try to get my client out of the situation. Other things can cause a negative emotional reaction as well. The location of a home or certain items in the home – all kinds of random things can cause a negative emotional reaction. As your REALTOR®, it is my job to pay attention, notice these things, and try to avoid repeating the situation.

Sometimes it can be difficult for buyers to find the right home; you can look and look and look, but it may seem impossible to find exactly what you want. For another analogy, you have to kiss a lot of frogs to find your prince. As your REALTOR®, I will not give up, and I persevere until we find the home you are looking for. I believe that there is a home out there for every buyer. Statistics show the average buyer looks at over 60 homes. Often, when you initially begin working with a buyer, they will give you a laundry list of things that are important to them in a home and/or neighborhood. However, after working with them, you start to realize that some of those things aren't as important as they initially thought, or other things become even more important to them, or the order of importance changes.

Some buyers are not forward-thinking, and, when they look at homes, they don't see or think long-term about where they may be in their life several years down the road. What may be important then, may be different then today. For instance, newly-weds, or recent college graduates, may not be thinking ahead to the potential of a growing family or aging parents; however, that can be important when you're considering the size of a home or the number of bedrooms and baths, and the school district. Neighborhood trends, zoning restrictions, or changes, are all important, but many buyers do not think about these things.

Oftentimes people don't think about the resale value either because they are so excited about the purchase. Fifty to sixty years ago, people would purchase a home and stay in the home for their entire lifetime. They would purchase a home, raise a family there, and stay in the home after they retired. Homes were smaller, people lived simpler lives, and were satisfied staying in one place. Things have changed; people do not stay in their homes as long as they used too. People stay in homes for a much shorter period of time, and move as their home needs change. It is important, as your REALTOR®, that I place you in a home that meets your needs, and that re-sell is always considered.

As your REALTOR®, I always consider resale value and ensure you are buying a home with excellent potential for resale, assuming that you listen to me. One of the worst things that can happen is for a person to buy a home that is impossible to resell. It is important to know the neighborhood and whether it is on the rise or going down, as well as who is moving into the area. Also, important things to know are trends in the economy, the local business developments, and current property values and whether they are increasing or decreasing. All of these things are important factors in purchasing a home and thinking about when looking forward to resell in the future. Even if a person isn't going to resell their home, the value of the home increasing is important, as your home is your most valuable asset, and, as your REALTOR®, I would encourage you to purchase a home that will grow in value over the years.

I cannot tell you how many clients I have worked with who have told me that the agents that sold them their home encouraged them to purchase the homes, or do things they were not comfortable doing in the home buying process, or to buying in neighborhoods they didn't love. They trusted in the agent as an expert, and had some regrets for doing so. As your REALTOR®, I would never do this to you, or any of my clients. In one instance, the agent encouraged the couple to purchase a home in a certain neighborhood, insisting the neighborhood was on the rise and that the property value would rise. Sadly, the exact opposite happened with the home. When we listed their home, they had little to no equity because the property value had decreased. They had been completely misled by the agent. As your REALTOR®, I will never do this; you can always trust me to guide you in the right direction to make a safe and secure purchase.

I have worked with other clients where the agents that helped them buy the home didn't provide them with all the information they needed at the time they purchased the home. Not all real estate agents have the buyer or seller's best interest in mind, especially if they are working for a builder or a neighborhood, because they are looking just to sell the property and not help the person buying the home. Sadly, most people do not realize that, and, of course, those agents aren't going to share that with potential buyers, as they just want to get the sell.

I am proud to say that I have never pushed anyone to purchase a home they weren't comfortable with, or to sell their home for an amount they weren't comfortable accepting. I have had conversations and heart-to-heart talks with sellers about the actual value of their home, or why the price needs to be reduced or priced at a lower price point. Sometimes sellers think their home is worth significantly more than it is because they have a personal attachment. This goes into the emotional connection they have with their home. As your REALTOR®, I stay abreast of the homes for sale in the area of my listings so that you have my knowledge in your corner. I keep apprised of the comps. When sellers have an issue with reducing the price of their home, or understanding why their home is not getting the traffic they would like., I have taken sellers into homes in their area in the same price range to show them their competition, and what the buyer is likely looking at and comparing their home to. This can help sellers have a better understanding of the current market and what homes are going for in their area. This can be eye opening for sellers. Yes, this creates more work for me and takes time. As your REALTOR®, I make a commitment to my clients to go the extra mile, five miles, or whatever it takes.

Perseverance in the home buying and selling process is important. I believe, if we keep looking, we will find the right home, and, yes, it may take time, but there is a home out there even if we have to get creative to find it. I am not a quitter and I will not give up. In the words of Babe Ruth, "You just can't beat a person who won't give up." As your REALTOR®, I will never give up. We will look until we find what you are looking for. In selling a home, I get as creative as necessary to market the specific home. Every home is different, and a *one size fits all* marketing strategy does not fit every situation. Each home has its own character and personality that makes it unique. I like to find those qualities and focus on those in marketing the home. I never gave up or quit on any of my clients in my law practice and the same holds true for my real estate practice. I will not quit or give up on any seller, buyer or renter, and, as their REALTOR®, I am here to motivate, inspire, and encourage them to keep looking. I let my clients know that we will get through the process together, and we can have some laughs and fun along the way.

When buying or selling a home, you should be concerned about the quality of your representation and assure that you are protected in all aspects of the transaction, and that your interests are being handled securely. I assure all of my clients that I take care of every aspect of their real estate transactions in a secure, safe manner. I allow them a safe environment to voice any concerns they have, including if something in particular makes them feel insecure. A personal feeling of insecurity is something to be taken seriously and should be addressed. I always want to instill confidence so that you feel safe and secure during every part of the transaction. Safety is important to most buyers and sellers, and something I like to instill in my clients. As your REALTOR®, I will provide you the same sense of security and keep you protected.

Chapter 3

A REALTOR® Who is Also an Excellent Communicator

In the real estate business, there are many people that you have to communicate with, and communication skills are of the utmost importance. Being able to communicate effectively and develop relationships with people is crucial in real estate so that you can get what you want. Most agents have terrible communication skills, and many agents don't speak English well. You want a REALTOR® who can not only communicate, but can also develop and maintain relationships. I am an excellent communicator and have the ability to communicate with virtually anyone and everyone.

It is imperative to have excellent communication skills when managing negotiations. I continue to be amazed by the number of REALTORS® and agents that don't have any communication skills and are extraordinary difficult to get along with. The fact that a large number of agents cannot communicate in English is shocking. Then there are the arrogant and rude agents that make it nearly impossible to get deals completed. When a person is salty, unpleasant, or difficult to deal with, people do not want to work with them. I have the ability to get along with everyone – salty, unpleasant, mean, and nice – even someone with no personality.

One may think there is a skill an attorney does not possess; however, communication skills are one of the most important skills an attorney possesses. As your REALTOR®, you get the value of my communication skills which will serve as an asset for you. I have the ability to communicate with the most salty, rude, and non-communicative people, which is truly a gift. I have a way to make people feel comfortable and open up to me. Few people can do this, but I began doing this when I was young, and I have been honing this skill ever since. In my law practice, it proved to be invaluable, and the same holds true in my real estate career.

Early in my law practice, I learned I would be part psychologist. The fact that attorneys are called counselors is no joke, and has a significant meaning. I remain a counselor in my real estate career so that you can be counseled by a real estate expert and an attorney. If you are unable to communicate with others, you will not be very effective. People come to me with problems and the need to discuss deep personal issues.

Some of the issues were things you would not want to discuss with people, and often they were embarrassing. As an attorney, I have an attorney client privilege with my client, meaning a legal privilege that works to keep communications, between an attorney and his or her client, secret. The privilege is asserted in the face of a legal demand for the communications, such as a discovery request, or a demand that the lawyer testify under oath. This type of privilege does not exist in the real estate world, but I still carry this principle forward in my personal real estate practice, and I take this bond seriously in dealing with my real estate clients. I do not have an attorney client privilege with my real estate clients; however, I take my relationship with each of my clients much more seriously than the average agent. As your REALTOR®, and as an attorney, I am in an exceptional position to provide you, my clients, with so much more than any other agent or REALTOR®.

I have touched on this a bit previously but I cannot overemphasize the importance of building and having relationships with others. You cannot operate, live, and work in a bubble. I have always enjoyed forging new relationships with new people. As your REALTOR®, you will have this skill on your side. I have the distinct ability to get along with anyone. In college, I joked that I could talk to a wall, and it didn't matter that it wouldn't talk back. No matter who the person was, I had a way to get them to open up and talk, whether they wanted to or not. I enjoy meeting and learning about people from different backgrounds and lifestyles. In the practice of law, I encountered people of all ages, income levels, and education levels, and there is not a *one size fits all* way to communicate with people. There are some rules that hold true for everyone; for example, you get more with honey than vinegar.

Over my lifetime, I have been astounded at the number of times I have been able to reach out to a contact, friend, acquaintance, or person I have dealt with in the past, and they have been willing to help me. I want people leaving any situation involving me, to have a positive memory, and not a negative one. If a person comes to me asking for a favor or help, I always try to help if I can. If I am unable to help them, I try to lead them in the direction of someone who can help. To me, this seems like a basic life philosophy – the Golden Rule. However, we have all had the friend that we have helped or gone out of our way to do something for, and when you go to them asking for something, there is always a reason they cannot help. Takers.

People like that take and take, but never give back. Generally, people want to feel good about who they are and what they are doing. I think paying it forward and helping people makes people feel that way. It makes me feel that way. So even for my friends who are takers, I continue to reach out and help them. I may curse a little while doing it, but I still help.

The Benefit of Using an Attorney-REALTOR®

As your REALTOR®, I will continue to make positive impressions on everyone I encounter, and practice the Golden Rule. I will not be a taker, and I will assure the safety and security of your transaction.

Even as a young child, I was brazen enough to approach my neighbors to discuss adult things with them. I always had an entrepreneurial spirit and from a young age thought about having my own business. We had a lot of elderly people in our neighborhood and I knew they needed help with various things around the house. I helped my mom clean many homes. I decided to start my own company called *Kids Incorporated.* I made my own flyers and went door-to-door to all the neighbors, telling them about my company and the various chores I would do for them. I guess I've had an entrepreneurial spirit since elementary school.

The other kids in the neighborhood saw what I was doing and became interested, so I decided to cut them in on the business and put them to work. I allowed them to do some work and share some of the profits. I treated the other kids in the neighborhood fairly and they didn't mind sharing in the profits and continuing to work with me helping our neighbors. Even at such a tender age, I knew the importance of the relationships I had with the neighbors, and I wanted to continue them and maintain them. I continued the business for several years until I got a real job when I was 15. Even after dissolution of the business, I maintained the relationships with all of my neighbors and never felt uncertain or nervous about communicating or negotiating with them, even though they were significantly older than me. As your REALTOR®, my entrepreneurial spirit is part of the package.

I like dealing with the same people because I try and make relationships and friendships with the people I deal with. When I practiced law, the attorney on the opposing side had a different view of the case; however, that didn't mean that they were my enemy and we couldn't get along. Attorneys who approached their cases thinking the other side is someone to go to battle with, starts off on the wrong foot, and will make things very difficult. In those types of situations, the claims were difficult to come to a resolution. Typically, those were the cases that stalled, never moved forward, and never served anyone's interest, and the parties involved were usually unhappy.

In the law practice, it could be difficult to get along with some people, but this is a testament to my excellent communication skills. I make dealing with me enjoyable, and it is not a show or a trick, it is the true me. When you work with me as your REALTOR®, it will not take you long to see that I am authentic and always my true self. I believe in being authentic and transparent to people. I have always been like that throughout my life. I don't play *hide the ball*, and I always believe in being my authentic self. Transparency is very important to me in all aspects of my life.

As your REALTOR®, you can be assured that you will always deal with the authentic Hope, and you will always get that with me. Agents who play games with other agents or REALTORS®, will also play games with their clients. If they are willing to lie to other agents, why wouldn't they lie to you? This is a serious question. When people lie or are dishonest in one aspect of their life, it tends to permeate to other aspects of their life. Honesty is always the best policy, and with me as your REALTOR®, you will always get honesty – good, bad, or ugly, you will get the truth.

You may be wondering what *hide the ball* is. This is a term used in the practice of law that means that you don't tell the other side things, and wait to sabotage them at an opportune time, or inopportune time, if you are on the receiving side. I did not practice that way, and, in turn, I was fortunate that other attorneys typically returned the favor. This was part of earning trust and maintaining relationships with people. As your REALTOR®, I make these same types of relationships so that you, my client, get the best outcome possible. In the area that I practiced, judges did not respond well to these tactics and would rather not see this tactic play out in the courtroom.

Without a doubt, there were occasions when I was the victim of trial by ambush, and you will never forget those moments, or the people that did it to you. In future cases, with those people, I was always suspicious and knew they were the type who enjoyed *hide the ball*. Dealing with these attorneys was always more difficult and it was challenging to get work accomplished on a case. In the end, attorneys who practiced in this fashion had the worst reputations, were the most difficult to deal with, and were the least likely to get a case to resolution. They didn't have relationships with other members of the bar, including the judges, and never seemed to fare well for their clients. It is fair to say that their poor conduct had an overall negative effect on their clients.

In real estate, *hide the ball* is not an issue in the same way, but manifests in a different manner. There is obviously no trial by ambush, and I do not miss that part of the practice of law. There is always the feeling or fear that when you are working with a buyer, a seller is hiding something in the home, but other skills from the courtroom and my law practice, that I discuss later, help me to identify these potential issues. There are agents who play games in the way they communicate or make offers. To me it is obvious when they are being suspect in their communication, and I can out play them to get the information my client needs. To me, this is a form of *hide the ball*.

My legal career trained me for these tactics and I can always see through these deceptive techniques. As your REALTOR®, I use my intuition to ensure there is no trickery or deceit in the transaction. When agents attempt this type of trickery, I find it laughable because they are usually very bad at the game. Yes, to me this is all a game. Honest people do not act in that manner. Someone with the skill and education that I have does not have to reduce themselves to petty games and lies in an attempt to get a better deal.

For instance, I have dealt with many agents who will lie about having many offers on a home in an effort to try and get a better offer, or in an effort to try and get me to ask for less in due diligence. I love saying no to these people or ignoring what they have to say. I have had this happen so many times, and, after I withdraw my offer, the home never goes under contract, and it is clear the agent was not being truthful. I have seen this happen time and time again. I can tell when I am being lied to or when someone is trying to *hide the ball*. Situations like that do not get past me and do not impact my clients.

The people in real estate who behave in this manner are not subtle and are easy to identify. They have an air about them and automatically think they are smarter than everyone else. My favorite kind of people to deal with is those who think that they are the smartest person in the room, when in reality; my cat has more sense than them. These are the easiest people to deal with because I will let them think they are the smartest and that they know more than me. People like this like to hear themselves talk and will typically divulge too much information over time. As your REALTOR®, I will know when another agent is behaving in this manner, and I am able to turn the situation around and use it to our advantage.

Desperate people act this way. Often, by saying that you will walk away, is all that needs to be done. I have developed many tactics that have proven to be highly effective when dealing with these types of situations. I continue to find more ways of handling these types of people, and I never forget when I encounter such a person. These types of agents always behave in this manner, no matter what the situation is. It is their personality and the way they run their business. They are doing a huge disservice to their clients. As their clients' representative, they are losing deals for their clients, and making their clients look like liars. Even with people who act this way, I treat with respect and find no reason to be rude to them. I have my own version of a relationship with them, but I never forget who they truly are because I know I may come across them again in the future.

There are also the times that I see the name of the agent on the other side of a transaction and I know that it will be an excellent, easy transaction because I have a relationship with the person, and we have worked so well together in the past. Knowing that a person has a level head, is honest, ethical, and has the best interest of their clients in mind, means we will have a smooth transaction. I work hard to maintain an excellent reputation as a REALTOR® and an attorney, and I can confidently say that I still have that reputation. I repeatedly dealt with the same attorney over and over in my law practice. Since leaving the practice of law, I remain in touch with many of the attorneys I practiced with over the years. I have listed and sold many of their homes and helped them find new homes. It feels good to know they have confidence in me as an attorney and as their REALTOR®.

There may be more REALTORS® than attorneys, but I continue to come across the same REALTORS®, over and over, as well as other professionals involved in the real estate community. For example, I regularly interact with loan officers, inspectors, HVAC people, plumbers, closing attorneys, and the list goes on and on and on. There are so many different types of professionals involved in a real estate transaction, and every transaction is different. The better relationship one has with these people, the easier and quicker it is to get things done, and the more satisfied my buyers and sellers are – and the happier my life is as a REALTOR®. With me being your REALTOR®, you receive the benefits of my relationships with so many others.

Every day, I continue to form more and more relationships and strengthen the bonds I have with my other contacts.

In real estate, part of the way that I do that is by giving feedback. Feedback is highly valuable and important in the real estate community. I always give feedback. I am honest with my feedback, but not cruel. Sometimes it isn't even something in the home you are showing, but it can be the massive dog next door that won't stop barking. Maybe the house is dirty, or filled with clutter. Whatever it is, I am honest. There are so many agents who do not return the favor and give feedback, which is so frustrating. As the listing agent, you have nothing to take back to your seller to say, "Here is what they thought," – good, bad or indifferent.

As your REALTOR®, I can assure you that I will always give feedback, and other agents return that favor. If 15 people come through and they all say the price is too high, obviously you need to have a conversation about reducing the price. It is a common courtesy to provide feedback, even though so many agents do not do this. There is nothing you can do to change these people. You won't refuse to let them see your listing, but you will remember those agents as being ones who never leave feedback. This does not go a long way in helping those agents with any listings they may get in the future. Do unto others – leave me feedback and I will return the favor. To many, this may seem like a small thing, but I assure you this is a huge deal in the real estate community.

Obviously, taking people into homes is a large part of what REALTORS® do, and, if it is your listing, you want to know what potential buyers think of the home – good, bad or ugly. The agent who has listed that property always wants feedback. Did the home show well? What do you think of the price? Is your client interested? Want to make an offer? There are other things that can be equally important, like the way the home smells, and curb appeal; many small things can make a huge difference. When you are selling a property, it can be increasingly frustrating when you have agents who will not provide any feedback. You have no idea why they didn't like the property. Having someone else come into the home and give you feedback that you can provide to the sellers can be very helpful. If you get people saying the same thing over and over, you can have your sellers address the issue if necessary. Your clients will appreciate this.

In real estate and law, clients often want guidance and hand-holding. As your REALTOR®, I will always be there to give you this guidance to instill security in your transaction. My clients are dealing with large life decisions involving a significant amount of money and emotion. In my law career, my clients were typically dealing with a traumatic event that took place in their life, changing them forever. A home is usually the person's largest asset, and no matter the value of the property being purchased or sold to that person, it is a large sum of money. It is important to keep this in mind when dealing with people and knowing that each individual is different. Some people you can talk too bluntly and straightforward, and that is what they need and prefer, while others you need to handle more delicately. There is not a one size fits all attitude, or way, of communicating with people. So often people try and handle everyone in the same way, and those people are not effective communicators. With me being your REALTOR®, you will get a highly effective communicator working for you.

You must be able to read people, especially when working with couples, because two different people can respond to language and words differently. Knowing how to say something and when to say it in the best tone for it to be heard, received, and digested, can be tricky. When giving a person legal advice or real estate advice, it is not my job to tell someone what to do and how to do it. I believe it is my duty to give them sound advice on the decisions they are considering and making, and assure that they know all the factors, and are aware of potential outcomes, as well as having all questions and concerns answered.

People come to me as an expert, and as their REALTOR®, and as an attorney, I provide them with the information they need, to make the best decision possible. I love that I am an expert. I want you to come to me with questions. I want to tell you what I know, and if I don't know the answer, then I will get the answer. In making huge decisions, people need to be well informed and feel confident they are making an educated decision, and a good decision. I want my clients to feel comfortable with the decisions that they make.

Being able to communicate effectively and develop relationships is crucial in real estate. One may think this is a skill an attorney does not possess; however, I think this is a crucial skill for an attorney as well. In fact, communication skills are of the utmost importance in the practice of law. I have touched on this a bit previously but I cannot overemphasize the importance of building and having relationships with others. I am able to get along with anyone. In college, we joked that I could talk to a wall. Now, whether it would talk back or not, it didn't matter. There's something about meeting new people and learning about them that I enjoy. The other important thing about conversations and talking, is listening to what the other person is saying as well. People like to talk, and when they talk, they want to be heard.

Oftentimes, REALTORS® and attorneys do not listen, and what is said goes straight past them. They will ask a question, but had they been listening, the question had just been answered. That is one of my pet peeves; just listen to what I have said. People who do not listen, or passively listen, annoy me. Don't act like you're interested if you don't care what I have to say, or don't ask a question if you do not care what the answer is. If what I say is not important, talk to someone else. For some reason, things like this stick with me, and frustrate me. As your REALTOR®, I can assure you that I will always listen to you, and hear your concerns.

Feeling heard is important, and people want to know they are being listened to. I remember when people ask me the same question over and over again. I always want to re-direct and do the same thing back to them but I have never had the guts to do it. Maybe one day. This goes back to the Golden Rule of treating people the way I want to be treated. I want people to listen to me when I speak, so I afford people that same thing. One of the main complaints people have about their agents is that they do not listen to them.

When I practiced law, there was one attorney who I worked with many times over the years, and, every time we worked together, this attorney introduced himself as though we had never worked together. It annoyed me so much. It came off as a superiority thing to me. There was no way this attorney didn't know me, or who I was. We practiced law together for over a decade in the same courtrooms! Apparently, I was not the only person this was done to by this particular attorney. I don't know if the attorney did this to me to specifically to annoy me or if they were just that dense that they really didn't remember ever meeting me or any of the continuing legal education seminars that I spoke at. Either way, it was incredibly rude and I thought it made the attorney look stupid.

Don't get me wrong; there have been times that I will not remember a person's name, but I am pretty good at remembering people's faces. I'll look at them and know that I know them from somewhere, but I can't place where or their name. This happens a lot when you have lived in the same area your entire life. You constantly see somebody that looks familiar and there's a good chance that you went to school with them at some point, or they are someone's parent. Just the other day at Costco, I ran into a friend from high school I had not seen in over 15 years. But when you've seen the person ten-plus times, in nine months – seriously?

There is more to listening than just not asking them a question about what they just said, or asking the same question over and over. You need to actively listen to what somebody says. You can listen to somebody all day but not really hear what they say. As your REALTOR®, I promise to actively listen to you, my client, and hear what you say. I may ask additional questions about what you say to get further information, but I will be listening. Sometimes you have to read between the lines of what a person says. People can have trouble articulating exactly what they want or mean, and it's important to be able to read between the lines to understand what they mean. They are not intentionally misleading you but everyone is not an excellent communicator. Some people are overly verbose and have way too much to say without saying anything important or answering the question asked. I am excellent at reading between the lines, which is a huge benefit to you my client. But you cannot always just let people keep talking.

In my law practice, clients would often want to tell me way too much information about things I didn't want to know. There were different types of clients. With some, it was like pulling teeth to get information – information that I absolutely had to have for their case. Then there were clients who wanted to tell you everything from their birth to present day in great detail, which was over the top, and more than I could ever want. Sometimes, you just have to learn to cut people off and say enough is enough. This will benefit everyone. In order to get the information you need, you must be able to know what questions to ask.

As I said, you can't just let people talk because they will either tell you little to nothing, or overload you with information that is not necessarily what you need or want. I know the questions to ask and as your REALTOR®, you will receive that benefit. As I have said before, I know how to get to the heart of the matter and ask the right questions, but I am also one of the best listeners you will ever meet. Hearing the needs of a client is important, but not all agents are on that same page. They will just try and get by on next to no information and just wing it, but not me. As your REALTOR®, I need to know certain things from you, my client, and will listen to you when you provide me with the information.

Different people communicate in different ways and like to receive information in different ways. Again, there is not a *one size fits all* way of communicating. How does the person want to be communicated with? This may seem like a silly question, but in this day and age, with so many different mediums, we can communicate with people in their preferred method. What am I talking about? Do they want to communicate over the phone, or by email or text message. There are so many ways now to communicate, and some people prefer one method to another. As your REALTOR®, I will try and communicate in the way that makes sense for you, the client.

You must take into consideration how they like to communicate and how they receive information. The age of the person can often determine how they want to receive information. Millennials can text 1000 word a minute, so texting with them can be appropriate. However, older people may prefer an old fashioned phone call. I actually have a client who still has a home phone that I call. I am not judging. If you call the person's cell phone, they will not answer. Same holds true with my millennials; they don't answer their phones unless it is a text message. My, how things have changed. Later in the book, I will get into the importance of technology, but this is a perfect example of how an agent, who does not know how to text, would not be a good match for someone that likes to communicate primarily via text message.

Not only is the relaying of information important, but the timing of giving information, is also important in law and real estate, particularly in real estate when you are dealing with tight deadlines. As your REALTOR®, with my legal background, I am fully aware of the importance of time deadlines and I always act accordingly to assure the deadlines are met. Along those same lines as your REALTOR®, I may have to deliver news that is not what you expected, or maybe is not great. In my opinion, it is never effective to avoid telling people things because you know they don't want to hear it, and you don't want to deliver the bad news.

I've always believed in speaking the truth, even if you know the person does not want to hear it. Remember, as your REALTOR®, I promise transparency and honesty. People rely on me as their expert to tell them what they need to know. I have never believed in sugar coating things; just tell them the truth and shoot it straight. I've also never found it effective to delay the inevitable. However, there can be better ways of communicating things. For instance, some things should not be said via text message, but should be spoken, at least over the phone. In person is the best way to deliver some messages, but it is not always possible in a time sensitive environment. However, you can typically make a phone call, which, depending on the person, can be a better means of communicating than by text message. Text and email are what some people prefer, and may sometimes be necessary. If you know when the person will have questions or want to discuss something, man up and call them. Don't delay the inevitable. Delaying doesn't soften the blow, and can in fact make it much worse.

I never forget, as your REALTOR®, that it is business for me, but for you it is personal, which is okay. I have had other agents, and some buyers, get upset with sellers, and say, "It's not personal, it is business." I have to remind these buyers that it is personal for the sellers because it is their home. It is interesting because investors understand that it is personal for the sellers, but can just cut to the chase on matters. As an investor, or someone who's never lived in a home, it is a business decision. Dealing with investors is a completely different situation all together, and can make a real estate transaction more formal or colder, so to speak, because the emotions are not involved.

I like being the REALTOR® for investors. These situations are different, and colder in a sense. They make purchasing decisions based solely on money, and from a monetary standpoint. It can be easier to think of homes in this manner. You are not looking for an emotional attachment, but for something else. Does the decision to purchase the property make sense from a financial stand point? If a property is being purchased as a rental, are rentals allowed in the community where they are looking? If renting is allowed, is there a need for rentals in the area? What would be an appropriate rental amount, and would the buyer make money on the rental? There are many things that need to be taken into consideration in these situations. Another important factor is, after the closing, how much additional money will they sink into the home? What is the desired end result: flip, rent, or lease? For a homeowner who has lived in a home for an extended period of time, it is very personal, which is a very different situation. I am well equipped for both situations. I enjoy working with individual buyers and sellers, as well as investors.

Certain situations can make it even more personal and need to be handled even more delicately. For instance, if it is a family home where the parents lived, and the family home that has to be sold, this can bring up a lot of emotion; especially if it's a home that the person grew up in. If a family is going through a divorce, it is emotional. If the family is being relocated out of state, or empty nesters are downsizing, these are situations, among so many different situations, that make home buying and selling emotional and personal. Typically, you don't know what is going on with the other party so it is important to keep things polite and friendly, but keep your clients' emotions in mind throughout the process. My legal career more than prepared me for handling these types of situations.

As your REALTOR®, I realize the importance of how emotional and personal it can be for you, but it is my job as your REALTOR® to keep a level head, and keep my business hat on. You can be emotional, and I will remain logical for you. Moreover, I have the ability to communicate with you about the necessity of putting your emotions aside in order to be able to think logically about the sale of your home, the reason you are selling, and the end goal. When a buyer or seller cannot take the emotion out of the situation that is what I am here for. As your REALTOR®, it is my duty to keep a cool head for all of us that are involved in the transaction.

The communication skills that I took from the courtroom and my law practice, has helped me immensely in my real estate career. I am able to communicate with everybody involved in the transaction – the door man at the condo building, the city trash man, the attorney who does the closing, or a judge or doctor purchasing the home. I can communicate with everybody, and I am able to determine exactly what the individual wants and how they can help my client in the transaction. As your REALTOR®, I use my communication skills to benefit you during the entire course of the transaction. My communication skills, combined with my listening skills, put me light years ahead of any other REALTOR®, and will give you a distinct advantage in the home buying or selling process.

You never know who you're going to meet during a real estate transaction; therefore, it is important to treat everyone with respect regardless of the size of the transaction. A transaction where I don't make much money could lead to a more lucrative deal in the future. The relationship I build with each person may become very meaningful in more ways than just monetary. As your REALTOR®, I don't look at my clients in terms of money, but as people, home buyers, or sellers. This is rare in real estate. Many agents see each client as a dollar bill, and only care about how much money they make on a transaction.

I have become friends with many of my clients, and we remain friends and keep in touch with each other after the fact. People who only think of clients in terms of money, or their career from a monetary standpoint, are missing out on the big picture and some of the most valuable experiences and life lessons. I have met some amazing people that I would have never had the chance to encounter, at various events, because I put myself out there as a REALTOR®. Statistics show that, after a closing, most REALTORS® never follow up with their clients ever again. Not me. I have remained in touch, and continue to check in with them to see how they are and what they are doing. I do this because I care and I enjoyed them as people. I don't have to remain in touch with my clients, but I choose to. When you work with me as a REALTOR®, you will be getting a life-long real estate expert who will be on your side and available to you when you need me.

Chapter 4

What You Say Without Speaking a Word

You don't just communicate with people verbally. Yes, your words matter, and what you say is very important; however, you communicate in non-verbal ways as well. You have five senses, and when you're speaking with somebody, all five senses are picking up on things. Words matter, but how you say the words is important. How you articulate, which words you stress, and what you emphasize, can be crucial. If you stress the wrong words, you will send the wrong or incorrect message to the person, which can scare away a potential buyer. If you have a point you want to get across, there is a right way and a wrong way to deliver your message. I am unaware of any other REALTOR® who has the interpersonal skills that I possess. I have worked for decades on my interpersonal and communications, and as your REALTOR®, you will get my unmatched skills.

Body language is an important part of this, specifically your posture. I am sure we have all interacted with somebody who had poor body language, which is a turn off, making you not want to interact with the person again, or at least limit your interactions. We all know the close talker who comes in a little too close when having a conversation, or the person who just looks at you in a way that makes you uncomfortable, or the person who is just standoffish and cold. The average person is completely unaware of their own body language and the message it sends to others. We all notice other's body language without trying. It is human nature for us to pick up on these things.

Engaging people with body language and showing that you are interested in what they are saying can go a very long way. You send off vibes based on how you stand, hold your arms, tilt your head, and by doing so many other things. When you talk to a person whose arms are crossed, and they are looking at the ground or over your head, they send the message that they don't want to talk to you, don't like what you are saying, or just don't care. That type of body language can speak louder than the actual words coming out of your mouth. When you see someone standing like that, you may not even hear anything that comes out of their mouth because their actions/body language speaks louder than their words. People see you before you speak, and can instantly start to sense things about you. Even the look on your face can be telling. YES, first impressions do matter. You can overcome an initial bad interaction, but it is an uphill battle. As your REALTOR®, it is rare that I give off a bad first impression. I am very aware of my posture and body language, and control my body language to be appropriate to the situation.

Body language is important when you're speaking and engaging with others, and people will remember poor body language if it is off-putting. People also listen to the tone and manner in which things are said to them. People do not like to feel like they are being talked down to, or like the person speaking to them thinks they are smarter or superior. These types of interactions leave a strong impression and resonate with people. It is important to have the heart of a teacher when you are imparting knowledge and information to another person. As your REALTOR®, I will never talk down to you or try to make you feel inferior.

I talk to my clients – not at them. As an attorney, I obviously know more about the law than my clients. My law clients came to me because they needed help and needed an attorney to help them with the situation they were in. They needed legal advice. I never saw it as my job to flaunt my knowledge or be boastful that I knew more than my clients. It was my job to teach them and protect their interest, but I also tried to educate them in the process so they would understand why things were important and what was going on in the process. I am the same way in my real estate practice. When I work as your REALTOR®, if you ever have a question or want to know why things are happening, or why certain things are needed, I want you to know that you can ask. I do have the heart of a teacher, and I want to educate you in the process.

I brought this passion for teaching people, from my law practice. The legal process can be slow, convoluted, and difficult to understand. As your REALTOR®, I want to put your mind at ease about any concerns you may have. I don't want to be the person who tells their clients to do things "because I said so." I try to do that with my kids too. When I catch myself saying "because I said so" to my kids, I try to rewind and state a reason as to why I have asked them to do what I have asked. Sometimes "because I said so" is the reason why I need my kids to do something; however, in the practice of law and real estate, there is usually a legal reason, or a good reason, why I need a person to do something.

Typically, I can explain and educate the person that what I am asking for is important. I have the heart of a teacher and I like teaching others. You want a REALTOR® who has the heart of a teacher to help guide you in the process. I believe that people like to be informed in the process, and don't usually like to be told what to do. I know I don't like to be told what to do, and when someone tells me what to do, it will make me want to do the opposite, or do nothing at all – not the right attitude, but pure human nature. As humans, we respond to people based on instincts towards others. This is another reason it is so important to teach people instead of telling them what to do, because it is the way I would like to be treated.

Facial expressions may seem like something silly or unimportant, but they also matter and are similar to posture. A facial expression can relay a hundred words without a single word ever being uttered. Think back to when you were a child. I am sure that your mother or father had a glance or stare that they could shoot your way, and you knew they meant business. If you didn't do, or stop doing, whatever they wanted at that moment, you would be in trouble. That one glance said as much as a thousand words. The same holds true in real estate; the expression on a person's face is very important.

For those of you who are married or in relationships, you can more than likely read the body language of your significant other. You know when they are mad by the way they speak to you or don't speak to you, as well as by the tone and inflection in their voice, their body language, or the withdrawal of affection. If you do not know the non-verbal cues of your significant other, you need to learn them, or get ready for many cold nights. The inflection in a person's voice, or the way they say something, can be very telling. I discuss this in detail when I talk about negotiating.

All of these non-verbal interactions strike a chord with people in any situation. It is easier to identify in personal relationships, but they also matter with acquaintances, clients and strangers. You have an immediate reaction to someone when you meet them, and they have a reaction to you before anything is ever said, based on the way you hold yourself, the look on your face, and your physical presentation. This is human nature. Actually, I think it is also animalistic. My dog and cat do the same thing. They size up other animals, and each other. After sizing each other up, they then approach each other in a purely physical manner. Perhaps all species judge each other by appearance. In the words of Yoda, "Size matters not. Look at me. Judge me by my size, do you?" Yes, Yoda, we all judge each other based on size, and the way we look.

As your REALTOR®, when I hold an open house, all of these things are important to me, and the way I communicate with a potential buyer is very important. The way I look, and the way the home looks, are both important. The way I interact with the potential buyer is also important. Moreover, it is also important for me to read these same signals from the people coming in the home to determine their interest level. I need to be able to read their body language to ensure that I am conversing with them in a manner that they are comfortable with, and to provide them the information they need in order to feel informed.

The Benefit of Using an Attorney-REALTOR®

If someone is at an open house and is not interested in the home, but someone else is present and is very interested, then that is the person I need to spend my time speaking to. As your REALTOR®, I am well aware of the importance of sizing up people at the open house and determining who has the most interest in the home. At your open house, it is also very important for me to give off all the appropriate non-verbal cues to the people attending the open house, and not to come off as overbearing.

Real estate is sales, and you don't want to be that pushy salesperson or seem like the telemarketer that someone wants to hang up on and doesn't want to speak to. REALTORS® have a terrible reputation, and they have earned that reputation by being overly pushy and aggressive with people, and making people uncomfortable. They'll hound and hound and hound a person, and all they ever talk about is buying and selling homes, and are always asking their friends and family members for referrals. It is as if they forget to have a life outside of real estate, and they come off as desperate. I get it. We do work on referrals, and I love getting referrals. It makes me feel good when somebody refers someone to me because it means they trust me and my work. But you have to remember to treat people as people and that they want to be able to communicate with you about other things.

I have held open houses where people have actually told me how refreshing it was that I was not overly pushy and in their face. They then go into horror stories about experiences with other agents and how overly aggressive they were at another open house. It always surprises me to hear these stories and I wonder to myself if those tactics ever work for agents. Nonetheless, I treat people the way I want to be treated, which is not by being in your face and overly aggressive. I give people the advice I would want to get if I were the one looking at a home.

If I don't think the home is well suited for a buyer, then I'll tell them that and I'll try and give them suggestions on other areas or neighborhoods that could possibly be a better fit for them. In the end, I want the person to be able to find a home that meets their needs and that they will be satisfied with. If you force a person into making an offer on a home, they will find a way to wiggle out of it, which will ultimately delay the selling of the home. Due diligence can be a bear, and I would rather not have an offer than have someone back out during due diligence, or later in the process, because that just wastes time for my sellers. With me your REALTOR®, you can be assured that I will not scare people off from your home, and I will provide them with the appropriate verbal and non-verbal cues needed in the process.

Along with body language, this may seem superficial but it is important to look like a professional and not like you just rolled out of bed. I may take this a little over the top since I am used to a law firm environment where we wore suits every day. I no longer wear a suit every day, but the bulk of my wardrobe is business appropriate. It is also important to know your client and the type of situation/environment you will be dealing with on a particular day. I have taken clients out to look at raw propertyies in the dirt, mud, trees and bug infested areas. On those days, I am not wearing a pretty dress and heels. I'm *rockin* my cowgirl boots and jeans. Some days you have to be ready to get a little dirty and be out in the mud. However, if I am meeting with a potential million dollar listing, I will rock some heels, a nice dress, or a suit. Not all REALTORS® are created equally and there are all types of makes and models, and people that wear all kinds of attire.

I have come to closings and seen other agents in tube tops and sneakers, which I think is unprofessional. Then there are those who come dressed *to the nines.* At the closing, with the agent in the tube top, the client of the tube top REALTOR® was embarrassed by the way their agent was dressed. They actually cringed a little when they saw their agent, and I think they were embarrassed by the way the agent looked. The impression I had with the tube top agent was that since it was closing time, and the transaction was over, she was just there to pick up her check.

It seemed like the agent no longer cared. It felt very cold. I am in the business of making relationships and remaining in touch with my clients. I guess the tube top agent did not care to have an ongoing relationship with the person. No matter the reason, the agent was dressed inappropriately and it left an impression on me, the buyer, the seller, and the closing attorney. The tube top agent is forever memorialized in my mind, and my client and I, from that closing, still talk about the tube top agent. You can be rest assured that, as your REALTOR®, I will always come prepared, dressed appropriately, and will not embarrass you by wearing a tube top to a closing.

The senses we have not discussed are smell, which may seem obvious, and touch. There are so many directions to go in with smell, but let's stick to the basics. You want a REALTOR® who has good hygiene, obviously, and I would hope that goes without being said. The larger, more important part of the sense of smell has to do with the way a seller's home smells. Certain smells can be a major turnoff for potential buyers. It is my job as your REALTOR® to be honest with you about the smell and to provide you advice on how to remedy the problem. Another part of the smell equation is that I like to make a house smell good for an open house.

This is not to imply that it smelled bad before the open house, but some smells are inviting, calming and relaxing. When someone is in your home for an open house, you don't want them to feel like running out of the house because of the way the home smells. You want them to like the smell and feel relaxed so that they can begin to envision themselves living in the home. I have several techniques that I use to induce a person's sense of smell that will make them feel relaxed and comfortable. The fifth sense, touch, is sensitive. You don't want your REALTOR® to be overly touchy with potential buyers – again, I assume that would be obvious.

The more important part of touch is an illusion. As a seller, you don't want people coming into your home and lounging in your bed while they are there, but you want to present an environment that invokes a potential buyer's sense of touch. Meaning, the buyer can see themselves living in the home and interacting with the home (touching the home). This contributes to making potential buyers feel comfortable. For example, in a dirty or untidy home, a person does not want to touch anything, and, typically, wants to get the heck out. A clean, well-kept home is appealing, and the potential buyer doesn't mind being in the home and surrounded by a stranger's things. This may seem silly and over thought, but all of these little things matter and the five senses play a large role, not only in selling your home, but also in dealing with others. As your REALTOR®, I want any potential buyer that enters your home to be relaxed and calm, and to feel invited, and, hopefully, ready to make an offer.

As your REALTOR®, I care what you think, and I have a client-centered and client-driven attitude. I go out of my way to help each of my clients, regardless of their price point. When I practiced law, there were attorneys who would focus or concentrate on cases depending on their perceived value of the case, and the same holds true in real estate. I have never operated in that fashion. I believe everybody deserves excellent representation regardless of the value of their case, the size of their home, or budget. A bigger budget does not mean a person deserves better treatment or a more experienced REALTOR® or attorney. Each person deserves an authority in their corner when dealing with large, life changing decisions. Treating people differently based on their socioeconomic status is frankly disgusting. Just because a person can't afford to spend a certain amount of money, doesn't mean that I will not work with them. Sadly, I am in the minority.

In my law practice, some of my smaller cases, or even some of the pro bono (free) work that I did, was the most rewarding. It was these clients who were always the most grateful and easiest to work with. These clients were often the ones who would refer me some of the best cases that I had. Getting a referral from a past client was the best thank you or sign of gratitude I could ever receive from a client. Knowing they trusted me enough to refer a friend or loved one to me, was always special. The same holds true in real estate. When someone refers someone to me, it warms my heart because they know that I will take care of that person and save them from the pitfalls of real estate. A referral means that they trust me enough to refer someone else to me, in order to help with one of the largest decisions and purchases they will ever make. They refer their friends and loved ones to me because they know they will be safe and secure in my hands.

Many agents are not client-centered, but are solely focused on the sale or buy. They just want to close the deal, when that is NOT what always matters most to the client. Closing the deal does matter to the real estate agent because that is how they get paid. Buyers and sellers have much larger concerns such as the bottom line, how much money will come out of their pocket, how old is the roof, or whether the new paint job is hiding something. If the agent, lawyer, or whoever you are working with, fails to recognize what is important to you, the buyer or seller, you need to fire whoever you are working with and find someone else. An agent who is only concerned with their own personal pocket will not be on the lookout for pitfalls, or anything else that can get buyers and sellers in trouble down the road, which can lead to severe, expensive consequences. As your

REALTOR®, I can assure you that your needs and concerns are my main priority. I care what matters to you, and knowing what is important to you makes me a better REALTOR®. Visit my website at www.hoperiesattorneyrealtor.com for a list of things to look for when buying a home.

Having a client-centered advocate is important. In fact, it's so important that, until you have somebody who is truly client-centered, only then will you realize the difference. It is when a person takes the time to inquire about you and how things are with your family and your day, as well as taking the time to assure that you are comfortable in the process, and answering all questions and letting you know that we will get through the process together. As your REALTOR®, I inquire about these things because I care and want to ensure that you are well informed and comfortable during the home buying and selling process.

Sure, tough love is sometimes necessary, but an important part of tough love is in the delivery of the message. You can deliver a difficult message, but if delivered in the appropriate manner, the blow can be lighter without you coming off as a complete jerk. A client-centered advocate, with the heart of a teacher, knows the best way to deliver difficult messages. Sadly, this type of person is hard to find. As an attorney-realtor, I am very well-trained and capable of handling these types of situations. As your REALTOR®, I promise honesty, but I also promise if the message is not necessarily one that you want to hear, I will be gentle in my delivery.

I have seen, over and over, in my law practice and in real estate, agents and attorneys who push their clients into doing things that the attorneys and agents want them to do. NOT necessarily what the client wants to do, and not necessarily what is best for the client. People who force their clients to do things are self-centered and self-serving, and are not serving anyone but themselves. When a person pressures someone else to do something whether they want to do it or not, that is bullying. Anyone who will bully you into doing anything is not worthy of your time, and you should not continue to work with that person. I have seen agents who talk down to their clients or make their clients feel that they don't have a choice.

As your REALTOR®, I will never force you into a decision. I will always give you guidance and sound advice, but the decision is up to you. I will tell you if I do not agree with your decision, but I will not try and change your mind. Agents and attorneys, who tend to push their clients into doing certain things, do it for monetary reasons. They want to move through things quickly. More clients, in their eyes, equal more money. Money is what drives many people. In my opinion, in the long run, if the client is happy, and it is a better resolution for all parties, it is a win-win.

Chapter 5

Everything in Life is Negotiable

As your REALTOR®, I will negotiate an unbelievable deal for you. I always joke that everything in life is negotiable; however, I really think that is true. As an attorney, I negotiated EVERYTHING. People don't think of things as negotiation, when in fact they are negotiating. The date when something will take place, what questions would be allowed, where a meeting will take place, who will go first, how much of a response will suffice for an answer – all of these things are negotiations. Some people see things as conversation – I see it as an opportunity to negotiate. Yes, I said opportunity. I look forward to negotiations because it is a strength of mine. I can negotiate with a person without the other person knowing we are negotiating. There are so many opportunities in life that people do not take advantage of, but I do my best to not let these pass me by.

In the negotiation process, small things are important and can make a significant difference. The non-verbal cues are of high importance in negotiating. When emphasis is not on the words one speaks, a person's tone and body language are all key factors. The way you say things and the words you use are of significant importance. I have touched on this before but delivery of a message is highly important. I have been in every type of negotiation imaginable and have dealt with a myriad of different types of negotiators. I trained internationally to learn how to negotiate. I doubt any other REALTOR® can say the same thing. In fact, most agents have no formal training in the art of negotiation. With me as your REALTOR®, you will have an internationally trained negotiator working for you.

I understand the significance of the delivery of a message, and, if you fail at the delivery of your message, the entire negotiation will collapse. There are so many examples of poor delivery, resulting in the message falling flat. We have all been on the receiving end of a person telling a joke, but without nailing the punch line, it just falls flat. When a person uses the wrong word or tone, or doesn't deliver a message with appropriate timing, it can be disastrous. Using just one wrong word, or not stating a clear message in the correct tone, will make your message fall flat. If this takes place in a negotiation, you are not going to come out on top. When I am in a negotiation with a person, and their message is falling flat, I typically cut them off and jump in with what I want. I take advantage of people who fall flat and fail to deliver their message. This is part of negotiating.

Another huge part of negotiations is listening to what the other person says, and being able to respond quickly, and on your feet. Listening can be just as important as what you have to say. People don't realize how much information they provide in normal everyday conversations. They just talk to talk, but, in the process, divulge a significant amount of information. Many of the qualities that I offer to my clients as their REALTOR® are useful in other aspects of real estate. My superb communication, interpersonal skills, and listening skills are key in my negotiation skills.

Most people typically love to talk and will provide a ton of information. Listening carefully to what they have to say can provide you with exactly what you need to know. In the course of what one perceives as a normal conversation, inserting a simple question can lead to a wealth of information. I use conversations as a way to gather information that is useful to me and the situation that I am in. This is not trickery or deceit, but me getting information and using it to my client's benefit. Knowing how to acquire information is a skill I possess, and I have skillfully crafted this tool over the decades. The more information I have, the better prepared I am to negotiate. As a litigator, my daily life was filled with negotiations. Settlement negotiations, trial strategies, negotiating with clients, attorneys, judges – you name it, we negotiate about it. This was part of the practice of law I loved because I did it in my everyday life. As an attorney, I was a professional negotiator.

People think of negotiations as bringing people together to discuss situations and come to a compromise. In litigation, people don't like to compromise because it can feel like a loss or weakness. Home buying and selling is full of compromises and negotiations. Compromise is a part of life which involves give-and-take. It is important to feel that you have not given too much or that you have not been taken advantage of. Taking advantage of another is another form of bullying that I do not condone; however it is part of life. In real estate, it is my goal for my client to leave the negotiation table satisfied.

When I practiced law and attended mediations, the mediators would almost always say, "Typically in mediations both sides leave upset and dissatisfied with the settlement." I never liked them saying that. It started the process off on a negative note. "Get ready to be unhappy," was the message. Why lead with that? Why set a person up to be disappointed? WORDS MATTER – don't lead with negativity. Be positive, and say positive words. Every time a mediator started with a negative statement, the mediation process was difficult, and we struggled to get things done. There was a noticeable difference when mediators didn't lead with the negativity; the process went faster and smoother. This is the perfect example of how much words matter. As your REALTOR®, I am very conscientious of the words I use in negotiations. I am cognizant of my tone, my delivery, and how the person on the other side receives what I say.

In real estate, I am able to negotiate in the way that I want to negotiate. No one else controls the negotiations. I can negotiate exactly what my buyers and sellers need, in the way that I want to. Better still, 99% of agents are clueless on how to negotiate, or that there is anything strategic to negotiating. This bodes well for me, and I use this to my advantage. Often buyers and sellers don't even know what is available to them, and I can open their eyes to things they didn't know were available. I love this part of real estate. It feels good to provide things to people that they didn't know they were entitled to; it's like having a cherry on top. This is a much better feeling than starting with the negativity of, "Be prepared to leave upset and dissatisfied with the process." Thinking in a positive manner can change the entire transaction, and can determine the course and climate of a situation. As your REALTOR®, I will negotiate to the fullest to assure that we get the best deal possible.

I believe in negotiating with everyone, for everything. I will always ask for a better deal, no matter what it is. I do this with everyone – other REALTORS®, agents, my friends, my spouse, people at the grocery store, and people at garage sales. If there is an opportunity to negotiate, I will attempt to negotiate. The worst thing that can happen is that you get a "no" response. So be it. At least you asked. My own children try and negotiate with me, and I always tell them I will not negotiate with them; I make the rules. I will not barter and bargain with my kids when they want something. If they need to do a chore or task, than they need to get it done. One of the joys of being a parent – I get to make the rules! If the worst that can happen is to get a "no" – and often you will get a "yes," or half a "yes" – why not ask. The word "no" can be very powerful, and a strong deterrent to many, but it doesn't stop me from asking.

So many people get one "No," and they never ask again, because they cannot handle the rejection. People fail to see that if you never ask for something, the answer is automatically "No," so you might as well ask because you are certain to get an occasional "Yes." The more you ask, the more confident you get, and the more often you will get a "yes." The more you get a "yes," or a partial "yes," it will build your confidence. By living by that philosophy, I have gotten a lot of "yes" answers, some partial "yes" answers, and, of course, some "no's." You just can't be scared to ask. Fear takes over for so many. You will never be a strong negotiator if you fear the word "no," or fear rejection. As your REALTOR®, I will always ask for things, even if the answer is no – all I can do is try. Rejection does not scare me, and neither does the word "no."

Not only is everything in life negotiable, but it helps to be highly persuasive in the way you speak to the person. Regarding body language and communication skills, not everyone is persuasive. Being persuasive is a talent and strength that I possess, and learned in the courtroom and in my law practice. Few people are as persuasive as me. I say this not to impress you, but rather to say that so often clients will want to tell me how to do my job. They will say, "Make this offer," or "Do X," or "Set this deadline." I do not like to operate in that fashion. I need to do things my way in order to make the deal work. So many times I have impressed clients with what I have been able to get them. I use my skills of persuasion to get what I want. Maybe that makes me sound like a spoiled brat, but it is simply a fact.

Being persuasive is a highly effective tool and skill to have in your REALTOR®. The powers of persuasion cannot be underestimated. So many people think that they are able to persuade others, but, in fact, no one wants to have anything to do with them. They just do whatever they can to get the person to be quiet and go away. Being persuasive is subtle. You cannot be overbearing; that is the opposite of persuasion. Real estate transactions typically involve large sums of money. When dealing with such large amounts of money, a person should want a REALTOR® that is persuasive and not afraid to ask for things.

Persuasion is not something you can teach; you either have it or you don't. Being persuasive combines a multitude of different things that I happen to have mastered. An important part of being persuasive is being able to read people and think on your feet. You must be able to anticipate people's responses, and always be a few steps ahead of them in order to persuade them to your side, or what you want. I can't give away all of my tricks, but the majority of people are not perceptive enough to be persuasive, or mistake persuasion with something else. Often women will try and use sexual undertones in an effort to be persuasive, but that is not persuasion, that is something entirely different, meant for another book all together.

I find that people find it easier to give in than to argue or stand up to others. Just asking is sometimes half the battle, but people don't want to ask because they are lazy or fear the rejection. I believe most agents don't mind getting their buyers to pay more money for a house because it means more money in their pocket, but that is not the way I handle my real estate business. I will always use my powers of persuasion, negotiation, and contracts to get my clients the best deal possible. Again, I don't fear rejection, and will always ask. As your REALTOR®, I will be proactive in getting the best end result for you, my client.

It is important to always know more than the other person, and stay on top of the real estate market because it can change quickly. In law, to get the best result for my clients, I needed to know the case better than the other attorney, or anyone else involved in the claim. I needed to know the facts, backwards and forwards, and, if there was medical evidence, knowing what the medical records did and did not say, and the opinions of the experts, was incredibly important. Having a keen grasp on the timeline was of utmost importance. If I was able to call the other attorney's bluff, or correct them when they misstated facts or evidence, I knew I had a leg up and had the upper hand. My in-depth knowledge of my cases is part of the reason I work so hard and work such long hours. It took a great deal of work to know my cases and clients, inside and out, and in detail; however, it typically provided fruitful rewards.

In real estate, the end result is different, but I always want a favorable result for a client. You may be dealing with a multiple offer situation, or with a seller who refuses to lower the price of the home, or a property that has some serious structural or foundation issues. Each of these situations can be handled best by a proactive approach. The same holds true for my real estate listings. I know the best and worst things about my seller's homes. In my law practice, I was always of the opinion that the best thing to do was to confront problems or issues with a case head-on, instead of trying to act like it didn't exist.

I feel the same way in my real estate practice. I need to know your home's highlights that will help sell the home, and the issues that may prevent the sale of the home. If something is going to be an issue, we need to be ready to address the issue and not act like it does not exist. How can we market the home with the problem, or is the issue so severe that it needs to be fixed in order to sell the home? Some issues are so big that I have to have an honest conversation with my sellers about whether we need to repair the problem, or sell the home with the problem knowing that they will likely get less for the home with whatever the issue is.

These can be tough, difficult conversations; however, it is imperative and necessary. In situations like this, the home concern WILL come up on the inspection report, and/or potential buyers will notice the problem, and possibly not put in an offer due to the problem. These issues can prevent the home from selling, so we need to address the problem quickly. Being proactive, and dealing with these issues, is the best way to handle these situations. Any good REALTOR® will walk around the house and notice the problems.

A good REALTOR® will also be honest with you and tell you if your home smells like smoke, or animals, or moth balls, which can prevent a home from selling. If your home is outdated, it will also drastically reduce the asking price, and if there is no curb appeal, it will prevent people from even coming in the front door. As your REALTOR®, I am proactive in addressing these concerns from the onset, and I will help you come up with a plan to address the situation. I make sure the seller knows that if the issues are not addressed, it may take longer to sell, and/or the home may sell for a lower price. I like to provide my seller with all the facts, lay out our options for moving forward, and let them make the decision on how they wish to proceed. The decision is up to them, but I want them to be informed when they make the decision. As your REALTOR®, I want to assure that all of your questions and concerns are addressed, and you have confidence in whatever decision you make.

I proactively solicit and market potential buyers that would be interested in the type of home in the neighborhood environment. Different types of buyers and people want to live in certain communities at different price points, and it's important to proactively solicit those people for your listings. The real estate market allows me to be creative and expand my thought process in order to get things accomplished. I have a creative mind, and in real estate I use my creative mind to create different marketing strategies for certain types of property. You cannot market every type of property the same way. A property in a downtown city, on the 45th floor, has a different audience and market then a suburban home in a *swim/tennis* neighborhood. These two types of homes appeal to different types of buyers, who do not necessarily respond to the same type of marketing. Each property needs a creative marketing strategy, specifically designed to sell that property. The first step is just recognizing that there is a difference in the marketing of these two properties, and that different types of buyers are interested in these properties. The next thing is knowing how to market these properties differently, and not just have *a one size fits all* marketing strategy for every property you list.

There is always more than one way to get to the desired end result. Many people have trouble seeing past the one way they usually do things. People get so comfortable with how they do things that they become inflexible or unwilling to change. There are typically multiple ways to arrive at the desired end result, but sometimes you must be creative in finding the route that will get you to the result. Solutions are not always obvious. As long as I know what the desired end result or end goal is, I have the ability to be creative in achieving that goal. Every situation isn't the same; I can come up with something creative, think on my feet and outside of the box, to achieve the desired end result. In my opinion, the worst thing you can do is give up and decide there's nothing you can do to move forward. So many people in life are stuck in their ways and are very resistant to change. People are incapable of evolving or changing, which is a disservice to their clients, and to themselves, frankly. I constantly evolve and look for the best ways to improve my techniques in order to be the best REALTOR® I can be for my clients.

As an attorney, you are always thinking on your feet, critically and analytically. Critical thinking is important when practicing law. I think critically and analytically in every situation, whether I want to or not. My brain immediately begins to work, analyzing and breaking down what is said to me. I do this in every aspect of my life. Practicing law for over a decade gives me a distinct advantage in the way I think. I'm sure some people find that annoying; however, I don't know how else to think. I analyze everything that is said to me, and my brain interprets things in a different manner than most people.

Whenever anyone says something, it goes into my brain; I break it apart, and I immediately look for weaknesses, where I can get ahead, or where there are holes. I do this with everyone, even my own spouse. It really drives him nuts. I give my kids a break, but only because they are little. I am sure, as they grow older, I will begin to dissect what they say too. My analytical mind will cause me to think about what is said before I respond. So often, people speak without thinking, and they speak when they really have nothing to say. This is when things get said that are the most revealing. It is important to have a REALTOR® who can pick up on these things and does not provide the information dump to the other party.

My critical thinking and analytical skills help me solve problems for my clients, on both the buy and sell side, as well as for my investor clients. Buyers, sellers, and investors have different needs and wants, and different strategies for negotiation are necessary. I can't divulge all of my secrets; however, in contracts and negotiations there are many things you can do to get exactly what you want and need for the desired end result. This can take place when working on a purchase and sale when selling a home, or during the due diligence process. The negotiations do not take place in a bubble, but they end up in contracts in the real estate world.

An important part of contracts is not only what should be in them, but also what should NOT be in them. If certain things are contained in contracts, it can lead to huge problems with appraisals which can lead to a person needing to bring a significant sum of money to the closing table, or, even worse, the closing being postponed or even canceled. This *minor* mishap can destroy a deal. For most buyers, the worst case scenario is forking up additional, unexpected money at closing. The worst case scenario for a seller is for a sale to fall through.

I have seen agents, who have been in the real estate business for 30 plus years, putting language in contracts that should not be there, and that would lead to these types of issues. The problem is that when this language is included in the contract, we often don't know of the issue until 48 to 72 hours before the closing. For example, all parties get the last minute big surprise that they need to bring ten thousand extra dollars to the closing, because their agent put something in the wrong place in the contract that screwed up the deal, or their agent did not catch the mistake because they are sloppy. I have seen this happen to other agents. In this day and age, lenders are looking very closely at loan applications, and at the purchase and sale agreements.

When the real estate market imploded and several lenders had to be bailed out, the lending guidelines became increasingly strict, and they continue to get more and more strict. Many agents have not stayed on top of the stricter regulations, and do not necessarily understand how the strict regulations affect the contract process and the purchase and sale agreements. Agents continue to do things the way they always have, which is the problem. The government and real estate industry does not want to go back to that time and have another fall out.

In an effort to prevent this from happening again, they are examining the contracts much closer than they have in years past. Agents who are not willing to change their old ways of writing offers may find themselves and their clients in these situations. The deals fall through and everyone is left starting over with everyone's time and effort having been wasted due to sloppiness. There are ways to include what you need in the contract as a whole, but there is a certain place to put the information. Where it goes makes a HUGE difference and can be the difference in a deal going through or falling apart. You may have to be creative in how to get the deal done, but where there is a will, there is a way. You can visit my website www.hoperiesattorneyrelator.com for a complete list of the GAR real estate forms.

The typical REALTOR® is completely uneducated on contracts, and has no idea the legal implications of what they are doing. They draft the documents to the best of their ability and haphazardly sign the *legal* documents; their actions can invalidate the contract. These documents deal with hundreds of thousands of dollars. A house purchase is typically a person's largest investment, and it is asinine that so many agents don't take the signing and completing of the legal documents more seriously. In fact, so many agents are unfamiliar with the laws and what should and should not be in these documents, but no one has ever questioned their knowledge. The average buyer or seller would not know what to ask an agent in order to test whether they know anything about contracts.

Whenever I question agents on why they have incorrectly completed contracts, they typically respond that they have always completed them this way. I can usually get them to agree to modify or change the contract to make it legally valid and not leave either party open to potential issues. I know that even though they changed the one contract, in the future they will go back to doing things incorrectly, and other agents will not catch the mistake. These mistakes open their clients up to invalidated contractual documents, potential lawsuits and the loss of significant money.

Many agents will change the documents as they go between the parties, as if it is no big deal, without the permission of the other side. This, too, invalidates the contract and the agreement. It is clear that these agents have no knowledge of what makes a contract valid and binding. These agents are completing invalid contracts that would never hold muster in a court of law. They are sloppy and lazy, and will never change. With me as your REALTOR®, you will be safe with me contracting for you. I have legal training and experience of what is and is not a contract. I do not take making contract lightly because I realize the importance of the documents and what can happen if they are not completed correctly. Few, if any other REALTORS®, will have the contractual experience that I have, since I practiced law for so long. Your sense of security is of the utmost importance to me when contracting on your behalf. You will feel confident in me, and sleep well at night, knowing you have an attorney-realtor on your side.

Chapter 6

A REALTOR® Who Will Fight for Your Rights

I am a strong-willed woman who will not be pushed around or influenced socially or morally. One thinks of this when they think of an attorney, but when I work with you, as an attorney-REALTOR®, you will be getting all the fight I have to offer. You need someone in your corner that will not be swayed by others, and is willing to stand up for you. You want this quality in your REALTOR®. I am a woman of integrity and I stick to my guns and what I believe in. I maintained this while practicing law and it continues in my real estate career. I am proud to say that I have maintained my integrity and always do things my way. I always stood my ground and was my own person.

Not only do you have to fight for your right to party, but you also have to fight for the house for which you want to ensure you get the best deal possible, and that you actually get the house. You don't want someone who is not willing to go the extra mile for you. Most agents are not willing to put themselves out there and ask for things for their clients. Even worse, they don't know all the things that are available to their clients, or what to ask for. Lucky for my clients, that is not the way I operate. I never hold back from asking for anything if it is to the benefit of my client, as long as it is something that is possible. I'm yet to figure out how to make the impossible happen, but, if I do, that will likely be my next book.

I am my own person and this is something I encourage in my own children. As a mentor, I always encourage my mentees to have the strength to say no, and stand up for what they believe in as well. "No" is a powerful word. Once you say yes to something you are not comfortable with, in my experience, people will continue to take, or try to take from you because they know that you will not say no. It is much easier to say yes then it is to say no. As an attorney, I was my client's advocate. As your REALTOR®, I will be your advocate in the home buying and selling process. I like being that person because I love to serve my community and make a difference. In my law practice, I was making a difference, but it did not directly affect my community.

I like working in my community; it gives me a sense that I am giving back in a meaningful way. I learned what community was from the neighborhood I grew up in as a child. I grew up in a small, four-sided brick, 1950's ranch home that was 1185 square feet. The house was small, but our yard was huge, and we lived in an amazing community. We knew all of our neighbors and they all knew us. I grew up having this strong sense of community, and thought everyone had the same neighborhood. Everyone watched out for each other, and, as a child, I felt safe in my surroundings. We knew everyone on our street, and, even as a child, I was comfortable going to the doors of any of the neighbors, for any reason.

In my neighborhood, we all waived to each other and spoke when we saw one another. In times of need, we supported one another, and in times of joy, celebrated together. To me, this is what community looks like. I felt safe in my community growing up. This sense of community was what initially peaked my interest in real estate. I lived in an extremely small home that had no air conditioning. On hot summer nights, I would dream about other homes.

Whenever I went to someone's home, I always enjoyed being there and seeing how other people lived. The area I grew up in exploded in the late 1980's and 1990's, from a residential standpoint. Once I was old enough to drive, I began exploring new subdivisions and touring open houses. I went into the homes starting from when the foundation was poured, to the framing process, and right up to when the home was finished. I loved going into the homes and seeing how they were constructed. Seeing homes in the framing process was an excellent learning experience for me.

I was able to see how homes were built, literally from the ground up. This was when I first began to learn about the building process, and there is a lot to be learned by watching a home being constructed from start to finish. What is even more interesting is to see how these homes look 20 plus years later – which homes have held their value better than others based on the construction, and what homes have structurally remained the most sound. I learned early on that all builders are not created equally. My passion for real estate has grown since I was a child. As your REALTOR®, my passion for real estate will be obvious, as well as my desire to help my community.

I like making a difference in my own community and giving back to the place that taught me what community is, and how important it is to have a strong community. As a mom, I want to pay it forward and provide the same sense of community for my kids. As I age, community has become more and more important to me. So has the importance of giving back to my community. I remain involved in my community and give back in many ways. I am involved at my kids' school, and I am a member of my local Chamber of Commerce. I give back as much as I can.

I have seen the metro Atlanta area change so much over the decades, but I have always been faithful and proud to be part of the change. I have an in-depth knowledge of the area that most do not have. I know silly things like shortcuts to the interstate, where the grocery store is located, where the best place to get a sandwich is, and, if you drive a half mile down the road, the gas is less expensive. I can tell you the best place to get Thai curry, a margarita, take out Chinese food, and where you can have an awesome kid's birthday party. With me being your REALTOR®, you will have access to all my inside information and tips.

As a REALTOR®, I am able to reach out and help my community directly and indirectly. I am helping people find a place to live and making it a home, and hopefully giving them a sense of community. I also get to help the local economy and tell people the best things about the areas they are living in. I can share my excitement about the community with them if they are new to the area. As a REALTOR®, I have the opportunity to give back to others and help people with one of the most important decisions they will ever make. If I can provide people with a similar community to what I had growing up, that would be an honor for me.

Becoming a REALTOR® was the perfect career choice for me. It allows me to serve my community, help others, and use my skills as an attorney in an invaluable way of servicing others. I take great pride in being an area expert, and my knowledge of metro Atlanta cannot be surpassed. It is highly unlikely that you will find another REALTOR® who has lived in the area as long as I have, and has the same knowledge of the community. As your REALTOR®, this is an invaluable service. Many agents will try and help clients in areas they are not familiar with and do not have knowledge about.

When agents come into communities that they do not know, or they are not familiar with, for a purchase or a sale, they are doing a disservice to their clients. It is a single transaction for them, but the purchase and sale of a home makes a lasting imprint on a community. I have seen many REALTORS® who come into communities and list homes with the intent of getting quick sales/turn arounds, but this effects the homeowners in the community for a long time. A REALTOR® whose only interest in the community is a quick paycheck is not an agent you want representing you. These agents are doing a disservice to the community when they come in and list homes for under market value. It short changes the community as a whole.

The agent gets in and out, but the community is left with the long term effects of a home sold for less than market value. As your listing agent, I will not allow this to happen and will not assist with decreasing home values. The old adage that a person's home is their largest investment is still true. People want their largest investment to gain equity over time, and not be stagnant or drop in value. Agents, that come into communities looking to get in and out with a quick sale, are not typically concerned with the long term effects of an under market value sale. If a seller wants to sell their home for under market value, a REALTOR® must oblige. Any agent looking for a quick sale is not someone you want representing you. If they do not take home values seriously, they have no business being in real estate. Buying and selling homes is serious business, but it is also important to keep a sense of humor.

There's no reason for the process of buying and selling your house to be dull and boring; I always try and keep the process fun, if possible. I try and maintain my sense of humor in the process. I want my clients to enjoy the process, and let me handle the heavy burden. If you cannot laugh at some of the things you see, you may go crazy in the process. Some things seem unimaginable. From hoarder homes, to the most beautiful homes you have ever seen, you just never know what you're going to see – so I always remember to keep a smile on my face.

The home buying and selling process can be stressful, but it is temporary. While working with buyers and sellers, I try to keep them calm and on task to remember that we will get through the process and we will get through it together. I believe all of my clients really appreciate the fact that I will laugh with them and keep the mood light, while taking my job seriously at the same time. I can joke around about something while still keeping my attorney hat and REALTOR® hat on. With me, as your REALTOR®, I cannot promise everything will be easy and smooth sailing, but we will have a good time, and probably have a laugh or two.

Not only will we laugh, but I always try to stay positive. Being positive is a choice. You have the choice to be positive or negative. So many people think that you are either a glass-half-full person or a glass-half-empty person. The fact is, the glass is refillable. You can choose to live your life in a positive manner, or a negative one. If you are feeling a little less than full, or are feeling empty, you can fill your glass back up. Yes, there are times when I can get frustrated. It is human nature. I will not act like it's always roses and pixie dust, but staying negative or upset about things does not make a situation any better.

You move on faster when you figure out that life is easier when you have a positive attitude. As your REALTOR®, I will always try and refill your glass when you are feeling downtrodden. I focus on my clients and do what I can to make situations better. Things tend to work out more smoothly when there is positivity in a situation. I try and always keep my glass full. A bad attitude will rub off on you. The negativity will creep up on you and make the process much more difficult. My job as your REALTOR® is to keep you in a positive environment and moving forward.

In my decision to change careers, I wanted to do something I was passionate about that would help me maintain positivity and be able to pay it forward in a meaningful way. I learned in my law career that negativity can eat you alive and take over your life. In my law career, many people had unrealistic expectations, and, no matter what I did, they would remain negative, and nothing I did would ever be enough. Even when we received the best possible outcome, it was not good enough, and they were unhappy. Some people could never see the good in any situation, and always saw the negative. They saw the world as a mean, negative place where people were out to get them. For a person like myself, dealing with this level of negativity, the people are vampires, and negativity is draining and taxing. The negativity will rub off on you if you are not careful.

Being a REALTOR® is hard work, but coming from a legal background, hard work is all I know, and it will never be too much for me. It is easy to understand why the majority of agents are not successful, and fail within the first several years of practice. In fact, the statistics are daunting on the number of small businesses that fail. Even worse, are the statistics for REALTORS®. Real estate is similar to the practice of law, in that you get out what you put in. Many REALTORS® try do real estate part-time, half-time, or practically *no time,* and think they can be successful. They do not invest in themselves or in their careers, and sadly they do not know what they are doing. They are doing a disservice to their clients and to the community. With me as your REALTOR®, you will be getting a full-time REALTOR® who works exclusively as your agent, and will not be a victim of the small business/real estate statistics.

Chapter 7

Eye on the Prize

In the practice of law, very small, subtle things can make a huge difference; therefore, it is very important for an attorney to have a keen eye for detail. The same holds true in real estate. Having an eye for detail is important on many different levels. For instance, being able to see small details when looking at homes with buyers. Noticing the small things can help with negotiating the price or terms of the contract. The same holds true for people who are selling their house. Small details can make the difference in getting a home sold.

An eye for detail is handy in contact negotiations. As previously discussed, leaving a word out, or adding a word or number can make a significant change in a contract or an agreement. You cannot learn to have a keen eye for detail – it is something that is developed over time, and a skill that is crafted and fine-tuned. Some people are incapable of learning this skill. They only see the bigger picture, or they are in too big of a hurry to get a deal done. As your REALTOR®, before I list your house, I will visit the *competition*. I want to see the other homes that potential buyers are looking at, to compare to my listing. I am comparing how competitive my seller's home is to the other homes.

It is important to see what homes, in the same price range, look like, and how they will show. This is a detail that most agents do not do because it is very time consuming. It is also very important to share this information with my clients so that they too are aware of what else is for sale in their area. Some homes are unique, and there are not any similar properties. If that is the case, I explain that to my sellers; or, I will bring photos and stats on the comparable homes, and be honest with my client about the other homes in regard to what things are more appealing and what things are less appealing.

This information is also important to know when you are discussing the listing with other agents, and at open houses. When you can talk in detail about the other homes that they have likely visited, or may visit, and how they compare to your listing, it can really market your home. When I do this, I can *talk up* my listing and sell the heck out of my listing. As your REALTOR®, I will provide you with this same service. I promise to do all I can to market and sell your home as efficiently and effectively as possible. The more you know the better.

When a property is unique, it may take longer to sell because it will take a certain type of buyer that will want the property. The same holds true for luxury properties (properties at a higher price point). Homes priced in excess of seven figures can take longer to sell, depending on their location and value. The market for who will buy a $10,000,000.00 home is much smaller than the market for a $500,000.00 home. However, an eye for detail is just as important in luxury listings.

Luxury homes have so many unique features and details. It takes a unique marketing strategy to capture these details. At Berkshire Hathaway, we have an entire division that is devoted exclusively to luxury properties, and the marketing of the properties. Again, there is not a *one size fits all*. The unique features and details in luxury properties are what make the property so special and are what will ultimately sell the home. This cannot be forgotten, even in the largest of homes and properties.

In marketing and capturing any property, a picture is worth more than 1000 words – hopefully it is worth tens of thousands of dollars. Pictures are the way homes and properties are advertised and marketed; therefore, they are of significant importance. I'm still shocked by some of the pictures I see on real estate listings. Some of the most seasoned agents post pictures that look terrible. In the photos, the homes are filled with clutter, and are obviously dirty, or the pictures are taken in such poor light that you cannot see anything.

Often the agent's reflection will be in the mirror, showing them taking the picture, or there will be an animal or a child in the pictures. Even worse, the picture of the outside of the home was taken from a car window, and you can see the inside of the agent's car! Worse, is a picture of the front of the home with cars in front, blocking the view of the home. No one cares about the car; they are looking at the house. I often see fuzzy pictures, off-center photos, or photos of, well, I am not sure what. I think capturing an animal in a photo is one of the worst offenses. Many buyers will not even visit a home if they see animal evidence in a photo.

In my opinion, you don't want any people, or animals, in any of your real estate photos. The pictures are for marketing! To me, this is beyond shocking. I always wonder if the home owners look at the listing and see the terrible pictures that have been posted. If they have seen the pictures, do they realize how bad the pictures are, and what a disadvantage this put them in? If a potential buyer is turned off by something they see in the pictures, they will not even want to visit the home. There are so many bad real estate photos, that there are actually websites that are dedicated to bad real estate photos. Sadly, many of the pictures on these websites are things you see all the time in the real estate business.

Pictures seem like a small detail, but they are of significant importance. Considering the majority of home buyers start their home search on-line looking at photos, these pictures are very important. Sometimes, there are listings that don't even have photos. If a listing doesn't have any photos, it is going to be skipped over. As humans, we are visual, and we want to see what is for sale. If I can look at 100 other homes with pictures, I am not going to waste my time on the few that don't have photos. Most people assume there is a reason there are no photos – the house is ugly.

Another small detail is that many real estate websites limit the number of photos you can associate with a listing. Many agents don't seem to realize that these websites sort the listing based on the ones with the most pictures; therefore, it is most advantageous to have the maximum number of photos in a listing. When a property is unique, or large, a normal camera cannot adequately capture the home or property. In these instances, a drone photo is the only way to capture the essence of the home; however, many agents will not go that extra mile for their clients, in order to save money. Again, these photos are a necessary part of marketing the home. I have a professional camera with a wide angle lens and several other lenses. However, many realtors rely on their cell phones to take the pictures.

There are other small details that I take into account when photographing a residence, such as the time of day. When will the sun be hitting the home at the best angle for maximum light? The weather is also important. Rainy day photos do not translate as well to potential buyers as sunshine day pictures. And I do not ever want any person, pet, or animal in my pictures. There are other items that all homes have, but, with my eye for detail, I notice and try to keep these OUT of my photos. Trash cans – I don't want them in my marketing material. Open toilet lids – or, really, a toilet at all, if I can help it. Dead or dying plants, any type of animal evidence, including, but not limited to, food and water bowls, litter boxes, dog toys or treats, or the dog bed or cat tree, are some of these items. How do I keep these out of my photos? Easy – move the stuff before taking the pictures, and then it can be moved back. Don't be lazy – pretty simple.

Another detail that I provide for all of my clients is not only that they get high quality pictures, but I also do a video of the home. You cannot capture everything on a picture, and the video allows you to capture so much more. You can see the flow of the home, have a better idea of the size of the rooms, and potential buyers have a much better appreciation of the home. Statistics have shown that potential buyers are much more likely to watch videos of the home than just click through pictures. My videos are not just a slideshow of the still photos, but it is actually a video walk-through of the home. With me being your REALTOR®, you can be secure and know that I will deliver the best quality photos/marketing materials for your home. I always want to assure that the photos are of the highest quality. If, on the day the pictures are to be taken, it ends up being rainy or overcast; I will take the photos, but come back on another day to take the outdoor pictures, if necessary. If I do not feel I can capture the home, I will hire a photographer to take the photos, but I have a select list of who I will use. I make sure they will take photographs up to my standards and will re-do the shoot if necessary, especially if it is raining when they go on the shoot.

If a home is listed when the front yard has brown grass, and stays on the market until the lawn turns green, I will update that photo. If something comes into bloom in the yard that makes the home look more appealing, I want to capture that and change the picture out. Any changes that make the home appear better; I want to photograph and change out the photos. You have to preview the home regularly, especially in the spring when flowers are blooming and the grass is turning green, to see if your photos need to be updated. You also do not want pictures of a home with Christmas decorations in mid-July. Photos like that have to be updated. As your REALTOR®, I try to stay on top of the photos of the home to ensure your home is being marketed in the best possible light.

Having an eye for detail as a REALTOR® is different for a buyer. Often, buyers will not notice small things in a house that they are viewing. For instance, sometimes buyers are so excited to find a home in a certain price range, in a particular neighborhood or school district, that they will be willing to overlook some potential pitfalls. The buyers will try and chalk certain faults up as something small when it could be a huge deal. For instance, things like the condition of other homes in the neighborhood, what appears to be a small water leak, cracks in the stucco, or what seems like sloping floors. It is always important to think about the time of year you see a home, and what conditions or things one would notice if you were there in the opposite season.

Many buyers do not see the small things, but focus on large things, not thinking about how the small things can add up to a large expense. For my buyers who are not nitpicky and don't see the small things, I take the role as their REALTOR® to see the small things, and point them out to them. I also educate them on the costs of repairing the small things, or, in the alternative, if they don't fix the small things, what can happen. As your REALTOR®, it is my job to educate you, my buyer, to all of your options and to ensure you are well informed. I want my clients to take ownership of their decisions when they make them. Noticing these small things can be important in the buying process when making an offer, and through the due diligence period as well.

Most agents leave the due diligence to the inspector, which is fine. If there is something you can do to help in the process, you should do it. Why don't most agents do this? I cannot speak for them, but I assume because of the time commitment, and that they are lazy. Many agents get a binding contract and believe their role is over until they show up at the closing to pick up their check. Many agents are in the business of getting in and out of a transaction as quickly as possible. However, there are so many things that I can do as your REALTOR® during due diligence to help with the process.

Most agents use this time to exit stage left. I am the opposite. I go out of my way to ensure that the due diligence is handled appropriately and timely. When I represent you as a buyer, I take the due diligence period very seriously to ensure all issues are addressed. I also want to make sure my buyers feel secure in the decision they are making. For my sellers, when they are going through due diligence, the same holds true. I do not let my sellers get pushed around by the other agent and allow them to ask for inconsequential items.

During one term of due diligence, there was an inspector who went into my seller's home, and this inspector was quite possibly the worst inspector in the real estate industry. I don't know where this inspector received their license and can't believe a reputable company ever hired this idiot. The inspector had a job and was in my client's home. It's the buyer's choice of inspectors and the sellers do not have a say. This character caught something plastic on fire in the home oven, filling the home with the smell of burning plastic and black smoke. The inspector did not come clean about the incident and tried to clean up what he did, by throwing the plastic remains into my seller's yard. The burnt piece of plastic turned into a sharp weapon-like object that their young son found and could have easily injured himself or someone else. Clearly this was a huge liability for this inspector and the company. The company's response was to offer to replace the spatula that was ruined – no apology.

The same inspector incorrectly quoted statutes and laws. Obviously, he didn't know he was dealing with an attorney, but, seriously, he was supposed to be the expert. His report was full of nonsensical statements that were so crazy that you couldn't even make sense of them. For instance, he stated that there was the possibility of fungus in the dirt outside of the house. Well, of course there is fungus in the dirt outside of the house. That is where fungus lives. He was not talking about mold, and he was not talking about there being anything INSIDE the house. There is fungus in everyone's yard. What matters is whether it is in the home. Seriously, this guy was a moron.

To make matters even worse, the idiot agent, on the other side of the transaction, bought into the report, hook, line and sinker. This agent wanted the seller to have an expert come out to the home and certify there was no fungus in the dirt outside of the house. Obviously, that was an impossible feat. Despite being insanely frustrated, I wanted to keep the deal. I called several mold and fungus experts and provided them with the report. All of the experts laughed at the inspectors *finding*, and concerns about fungus in the yard. The experts said exactly what I thought they would say, "Of course there is fungus in the dirt outside of the home. That is where it lives. What matters is what is INSIDE the home.

They could never provide something saying there is no fungus outside of a home. I asked the experts to call the other agent to discuss the stupidity of these statements in the report. They made the call and discussed with the other agent. Based on my follow up calls to these experts, the other agent did not get it. The agent continued to ask for the impossible so the deal fell through. What a huge disservice this idiot agent did to the potential buyers. Thinking back about it, even now, I cannot believe someone with that little common sense is representing people and *helping* them with the largest purchase they will ever make. That same agent never called me by my name, but always *Sweetie*. Also, unacceptable.

I could go on and on about this report and how insane it was, but now I just laugh at it. If you cannot keep a sense of humor in this job, you will not last. Life is too short not to remember this. Laughter truly is the best medicine, and sometimes the best thing to do in a situation is to laugh. This inspector frustrated me, but I also took the time to laugh at the guy's and the agent's stupidity. The other agent took the word of an inspector instead of an expert in the area of fungus and mold. The situation is so ridiculous that you have to laugh and move on. When that house went under contract again, there were no issues with the inspection report –no fungus. I have learned when dealing with unintelligent people who are incapable of grasping reality and truth, the best thing to do is keep your sense of humor and just laugh.

I will never do a deal with that inspector or agent again. I have blacklisted the inspector. AS far as the agent goes, they clearly have no common sense and will be difficult to deal with in any situation. As your REALTOR®, and expert, I remember these types of individuals and try to avoid them in the future. I did try and save the deal, but there was no saving the deal. I found out later, due to the agent being an idiot, the seller was not able to find a home and ended up in a rental. The agent made the deal fall through because of their own stupidity and association with an awful inspector. This agent was not informed or an expert. As your REALTOR®, I stay informed on the community and the real estate market, and advise you during the process.

I am well informed of what's going on in the area where my clients are buying or selling. If it is an area I am not familiar with, I will drive the area and become familiar with it. I am not the agent who sits back and waits for the buyers to send me listings before I make appointments. I go out of my way to try and find homes for them to see, based on their needs. If there is something particular to a buyer that is important, I keep that in mind in my search as well. All available homes are not necessarily listed on line.

As I have said, as your REALTOR®, I promise transparency and honesty. I have a high level of integrity and ethical morality. As a practicing attorney, I studied ethics and was held to high ethical standards. As an attorney, ethics were taken very seriously, and, if you acted unethically, you could face disbarment (loss of your law license), sanctions and bar complaints. There are plenty of attorneys who did not take this too seriously and were disbarred for unethical behavior, and rightfully so. Anyone who was willing to steal from a client, lie to them, or coerce them into doing something ethically questionable, did not deserve to practice law.

In real estate, there is no guarantee of a person's ethical morality. REALTORS® are held to limited ethical guidelines, but as an Attorney- REALTOR®, I take this very seriously. With me as your REALTOR®, you will have someone representing you who have a strong moral compass and a duty to uphold a high level of ethical integrity. In your real estate transaction, you want an advocate that you can trust and who you know will be honest with you. It's important to know that you can trust what a person says and that they will not lie to you or be dishonest with you.

When I hear lies roll off a person's tongue without any regard for the fact that they're not telling the truth, knowing that they can tell a lie with no thought as to who they may be hurting, it can be frightening. If they are willing to tell a lie in front of you, that likely means that they are willing to lie to you as well. People, who lie in one aspect of their life, typically lie in all aspects of their life. Lying is a personality trait that takes over a person's life, and it can be a hard habit to break. In fact, people may not even realize they are lying because they are so used to telling half-truths that they don't realize it and it becomes a natural habit for them. The half-truths and lies come out of their mouth the same as the truth. You need a REALTOR® who you can trust and will be honest with you.

It is important to have somebody representing you that has a strong moral compass and has a high level of honesty and integrity. When someone is representing you, they are a direct reflection of you, as your representative. If the person representing you is seen as dishonest or unethical, that is how you appear. When I practiced law, there were attorneys who had the reputation of being dishonest and having a low moral compass. Due to no fault of their clients, that reputation fell on their clients. Even if their clients were not hiding something, due to who was representing them, we second guessed their integrity. The stench of dishonesty is contagious, and this holds true regardless of the profession.

Chapter 8

Bright Futures – Let's Do This Together

As your REALTOR®, I like to think of myself as a full-service REALTOR® who will be with you for the long haul and into the future. You get my real estate expertise and my legal expertise. It is important to me to be successful and I always want to succeed. So I give 110% of myself in everything I do to provide for all of my client's needs. My law career, and lessons I learned in the courtroom, prepared me to be the best Attorney-REALTOR®. My legal background puts me miles ahead of other agents.

My legal career made me very inquisitive. My inquisitive nature, combined with my investigation and research skills, has proved very useful in real estate. As your REALTOR®, I use these skills to ensure that the property you are buying is secure from many potential hazards, and to provide peace of mind when purchasing property. I also use my investigative and research skills to make sure we get through the due diligence period in a timely and safe manner, ensuring all potential issues are addressed.

I begin investigating from day one when we start talking about the sale of your home or the purchase of a new home. If you are selling a home, I don't just pull a number out of the air to list your home. I do extensive research and investigation to determine the best price at which to list your home, and to get the maximum value in the shortest amount of time. That is the goal of most sellers – to get the most money in the shortest amount of time.

For buyers, it is different. Obviously, we are looking for homes that meet all the criteria you want in a future home, and sometimes you have to get creative with how you find the home of their dreams. I do not search only on the FMLS; I have many other tricks and investigative secrets that I use to find homes for buyers. With me being your REALTOR®, you get my tricks of the trade when you were working with me. I have been very lucky in being able to please people and find some amazing homes that were not listed on the FMLS; however, I was able to get my buyers access to the homes. Many of my personal *trade-secrets* involve the use of technology.

Many people are not comfortable working with technology, which in real estate leaves them way behind because everything is online. If an agent is not marketing online, they need to retire or find a new career. These are things that a person would never know or think to ask an agent, but are very important to the process of buying and/or selling a home. Technology skills may not seem like something important to a house hunt, but as your REALTOR®, I can tell you that technology skills are of the utmost importance. Virtually, everything is done online these days, including the purchase and sale of homes.

More and more people start their home search on the internet. If your home is listed for sale, and you do not have a significant online presence, you will be far behind all the other homes that do have a significant online presence. People will see many homes at the same time they are seeing yours; therefore, it is important to have your home stand out, AND be on the most websites. If you do not have a significant online presence, you will have more days on market, and decreased odds of selling your home. This is the opposite of what most sellers want. You want a REALTOR® who can market your home to the largest number of people. The more looks you get, the more chances you have of selling your home. This makes sense. Sure, a small online presence will not prevent your home from selling, but you want to have the most exposure possible.

One day, I received a business card on my door from a competitor REALTOR®, and she was boasting that she advertises her homes on 43 websites. I laughed when I saw her card. In my real estate business, all my homes are advertised on over 40,000 websites, nationally and internationally. An agent bragging about 43 websites compared to my 40,000 – I almost felt bad for the agent. Visit my website at www.hoperies attorneyREALTOR® .com for a visual of some websites where I advertise my listings.

Another important part of technology in this fast paced market, concerns contracts. When you are in a hurry or need to get something done, and it cannot be done in front of the person, knowing how to share documents and sign them electronically can help make or break a deal. As your REALTOR®, I stay abreast of all current technology available to REALTORS® to ensure documents can be signed timely and to ensure offers can be made. In this fast paced market, any agent not using this technology is in trouble and is doing a disservice to their clients. Waiting for formal, handwritten signatures can mean the difference in you getting a home, especially in a multiple-offer situation.

As your REALTOR®, I can assure you that I am very technologically savvy, and I have the backing of one of the largest real estate companies, Berkshire Hathaway HomeServices, who will market your home, locally and globally, which you will not find with another REALTOR® or brokerage. Berkshire Hathaway HomeServices takes marketing to a level that no other real estate company can offer. Anyone who knows anything about Warren Buffett knows that he doesn't go into anything half-hearted, and he wants to be the best at everything he does. So when I am your REALTOR®, you receive my expert knowledge and skills as an Attorney-REALTOR®, along with having Berkshire Hathaway behind me. You will not find a better combination in any other REALTOR®.

I use my technology skills to stay organized. You don't need to just look organized; you need to actually be organized. In my law practice, I needed to be as efficient as possible due to the high volume of cases I had. At one point, I had over 250 cases, which was insanity, and overwhelming to say the least. The best and only way to operate efficiently is to be organized. Thankfully, I learned early in my practice that organization was key, and I tweaked my organizational skills. I have since transitioned these skills into my real estate career.

I keep each client individually compartmentalized, and, even if they are a buyer and a seller, I keep the transactions separate. I have my own system, which may not make sense to anyone else, but it makes perfect sense to me! Berkshire Hathaway has provided me with so many resources that are a tremendous help in staying organized in ways that directly relate to real estate. In my law practice, I work with client software, but that is of no use in real estate. However, Berkshire

Hathaway provides me with so many tools to help me stay organized, and I implement my own systems as well. I like being organized, so, when I need something, I can easily access it.

There are many REALTORS® who are scattered and unorganized. I have scheduled showings and arrived at the appointment time to learn that the REALTOR® never notified the seller of the showing. This has happened way more than you would think, and is embarrassing for me with my client, especially if they want to see the home. If the person is never notified of showings, and the home is never ready, how will it ever sell? Seems obvious. Every time this happens, I go back and verify that I have confirmed the showing. If I were the seller of this home, I would be furious.

This can make you encounter several uncomfortable situations. I have gone to appointments where larges dogs have been out, keeping us out of the house. There was also a time when there was a sick child in the home; and the worst situation ever was at a condo where a mom was breastfeeding her newborn. Talk about embarrassing. Even worse for a REALTOR®, I have shown up at a home where the agent was so scattered and unorganized, they failed to put out a lock box. For their clients, they have done a significant disservice. Unorganized agents seem incapable of multi-tasking, which is what leads to these goofs and snafus. I can multi-task like no other.

I am capable of doing so many things at once, it is insane. The only reason I am such an effective multi-tasker is because I am so organized. To be a successful REALTOR®, you must be able to multi-task because many things will come at you at once, or at an inopportune time. You must be able to compartmentalize, prioritize, and multi-task in order to get everything done and meet all deadlines.

On several occasions when these situations have happened, my clients have gone on to write offers on other homes that same day, never returning to those properties. Only one time have I rescheduled an appointment where my client ended up moving forward with a contract on that property. It makes me sad for the person who hired that agent. I'm sure the other agent places the blame on me, telling the client I didn't schedule an appointment; however, I can honestly say I have NEVER shown up without scheduling or confirming an appointment.

This is part of being dependable. I have had clients who have cancelled on me at the last minute, but I always do my best to never be the one who has to cancel. I make myself as available as possible; however, I cannot always be available. When I schedule an appointment, I WILL be there, and I am dependable. You want someone you can count on when you are in a situation involving a large sum of money, or a fast paced real estate market. If you are unfortunate enough to end up with an unorganized, unreliable agent, the representation will be highly ineffective. I love to hear my clients say that they know I have their backs. My clients know that they can depend on me to take care of their needs.

I will continue to be successful in real estate because I continue to invest in myself and my own business. I train, and train, and then train some more. I realize the importance of learning from other agents who've been in the business longer than I have, and from new agents who have been successful using unique techniques. I keep an open mind and I am always open to trying something new if it can possibly be a benefit to my client. No matter the career, there is always room for improvement. I believe you can never over-invest in yourself. Berkshire Hathaway goes out of their way to provide training and education to their REALTORS®, and I take advantage of as many of the opportunities as I can. The day you stop learning is the day you die. With me, as your REALTOR®, you will know that I am up to par on all things real estate related, and will continue to learn to better myself as your REALTOR®.

I also maintain my law license and continue to take my legal continuing education courses, which I try to devote to real estate matters. I want to be as educated and well-rounded as I can be when it comes to advising my clients. I also stay on top of the banking and finance mortgage rates, as well as zoning ordinances and laws. I try and stay abreast of anything in the legal field that could potentially affect my buyers or sellers. I cannot stay on top of everything, but I do my best to stay ahead of the game, which is more than most agents can say. I would bet many, if not most, REALTORS® don't pay any attention to real estate/property law or the zoning regulations.

I could not be happier to have found a career that fulfills me as much as my real estate career. Growing up in an 1100 square foot home, I dreamed of living in a larger home, or just a home with air conditioning or a second bath. I never thought I would have the opportunity to help people find the home of their dreams, and serving people is such a great feeling. I have had the pleasure of helping first-time home buyers who range from recent college graduates in their twenties, to first time home buyers in their fifties. No matter the age, purchasing a home is overwhelming and is a decision to be taken seriously. I always take the process seriously and understand the importance of the situation. The feeling I get when I help people in the home purchasing and selling process, cannot be understated. By the time we get to the closing table, we have usually shared many laughs, and even after the closing is over, I like to remain in touch with clients.

Chapter 9

Who Is Hope??

What a strange question to answer – who am I? I was born and raised in Georgia, and have remained in the area during my adult life. It seems to be rare that someone is actually from Georgia anymore, but I am one of those rare true locals. Not only was I born and raised in Georgia, my roots run very deep in the state. My parents, grandparents, and great grandparents are all from Georgia as well. In fact, my mother still lives in my childhood home. I love my home state and my community. I want my own children to grow up in the community that molded and shaped my life.

Money was tight when I was a child, and we didn't have much. We lived modestly and my clothes were almost always hand me downs. My mom worked as many jobs as she possibly could to make ends meet, and at one point she had nine part time jobs. I had an older brother, Robert, who was my best friend while growing up. Robert and I always had to go with mom to her jobs because we were too young to be left alone. Mom cleaned the homes of our classmates, had a paper route, and worked as a lunchroom monitor at my school, to name a few. I am sure tagging along to all of these jobs instilled in me my strong work ethic. None of the jobs were glamorous, but they provided money to help pay bills and buy groceries.

My brother and I knew that money was tight, but we always managed to make ends meet. It was a miracle how the funds would find their way to us, allowing the lights to stay on. That is probably why I am still so frugal to this day. I am constantly walking behind the kids, turning off lights and telling them that we don't own Georgia Power, and putting empty pickle jars in the toilet to conserve water. Maybe my next book will be *Eleven Simple Tips to Saving Money!* Coming from such meager beginnings provided me with many important life lessons that few learn anymore.

I know what it is like to go without and to not have things. I learned that it's ok not to have what everyone else has, and not to be like everyone else. Individuality is a good thing, and, as I have gotten older, I have realized just how important being your own person is. Not having certain things can cause a number of emotions ranging from shame to sadness, but it will pass. Not only did I learn the value of a dollar, I learned how to stretch a dollar, save a dollar, and get the most bang for your buck. All of these lessons I have taken with me into adulthood, and try to teach my own children. Not having a lot of money as a child made me a saver.

I remember my mom taking me to the bank when I was very young, and opening my first savings account. I actually still have that same account. The bank name has changed several times, and I guess my name changed too, but opening that account impacted me. Having my own account, with my own money, was significant to me. I could save my money and even earn interest. I liked the idea of that because I was never a spender. I thought long and hard before ever buying anything, and I typically talked myself out of the purchase. Was it worth the price? Was it a need or a want? Was my money better spent on something else? Would I regret purchasing it? Even as a child, I had an analytical mind.

My brother was different when it came to money; he was a spender. When the Nintendo first came out in the US in 1985, my brother wanted one badly, but it was crazy expensive. It was $100.00, and there was no way he could ever save that much. However, as the saver, I had money in my account, and we decided to pool our money until we had enough to buy the system. It was 1986 or 1987 before we saved enough, but I remember the day we went to Toys R Us and bought it. They had it behind the glass case and it came with Super Mario

Brothers. I never regretted giving more than half the price for the Nintendo. I spent countless hours with my brother and the Nintendo, watching him play Zelda. Priceless memories.

I learned a lot of my frugalness from my great grandmother, Nanny, who lived next door. She was born in the 1890's and lived through the Great Depression, World War I and II, the Korean War, and the Vietnam War. She outlived two husbands, all of her siblings, and three of her children. That is not an easy life. She saved everything and found a use for anything you can imagine. She collected rain water for her plants, and used plastic bags to make pillows; she had over 100 Kentucky Fried Chicken buckets in her basement when she died. I'm not really sure what she planned to do with those, but she had them if you ever needed them. She taught me how to crochet, and the importance of patience. She also taught me that one needs quietness in their life at times, and the importance of service to country and community, and, when it comes down to it, few things really matter but your health and those who love you. The lessons I learned from her, I have carried with me over my lifetime.

During all of my education, I always took my schooling seriously; getting an education was important. I always enjoyed school and learning. I remember sitting at the dining room table and doing homework when I didn't have homework. If my brother had homework, I would sit with him and pretend to do homework. I don't mean to call my brother out, but I was definitely the better student in the family.

I remember my brother's first day of kindergarten and being envious of him. We waited for the bus and I watched him get on the bus and leave, but there is more to this sad story. As the bus pulled out, there he was – Cactus, my brother's beloved dog. Yes, the school bus actually ran over my brother's dog on the first day of kindergarten. I remember the day vividly. I also remember wishing I was the one going to school, and I waited at home for Robert to return home, wanting to know what he learned and who he met. Robert was not very interested in school. I always wondered if, because the school bus killed Cactus, this had led to Robert not liking school. RIP Cactus.

When it was finally my turn to start school, I was pumped. I had the same kindergarten teacher as my brother. Back then, kindergarten was only half-days. We took the short bus to school in the afternoons. I don't think we ate lunch, but we possibly napped, and then I rode the big bus home with my brother. It was awesome. My, how times have changed. Now kindergarten is ALL day and they have homework and projects. I probably would have loved that. All was great in elementary school, but things changed in middle school and began to be very difficult for me.

Eighth grade was a difficult year that molded and shaped my life in more ways than I could have ever imagined. Going into my eighth grade year, I would call myself a shrinking violet. I would let people push me around, and I let things get under my skin; I thought what other people said about me mattered. I was picked on relentlessly and had a lot of very miserable days and nights that year. In fact, looking back, I'm surprised I made it through the school year without quitting or getting held back because I missed so many days to avoid the bullying.

I think back to the few friends I had during that time, and smile. Those people will forever hold a warm place in my heart because they are the only reason I made it through the school year. The things that happened, and the things that were said to me, still affect me to this day. There was one student in particular that was so viciously mean to me, it has affected the way I parent my own children. I try to ensure my girls are never the bullies, and include everyone. I cannot bear the thought of my children ever treating any other person the way this person treated me.

It bothers me, the impact this cruel child had on my life. I live with it daily, even as I approach the age of 40. Sometimes, I wonder what happened to the bully because, luckily, we went to different high schools. I wonder if they have kids, and whether they are still bullying others. If they have children, are their kids being bullied, or are they the bullies? I also wonder if the person's parents knew of the cruelty their child imparted on others during the school day, and the joy they received from bringing another student to tears.

But, I have no regrets. I got through the year and moved on to Sprayberry High School – Go Jackets! I enjoyed my four years of high school and excelled educationally. I was able to grow my mind and challenge myself. I was challenged, and learned to think logically and critically. I had teachers who believed in me and made me realize anything was possible in my life, and I was the master of my own destiny. In high school, I began to believe the impossible was possible, and that I could do more, have more, and be more. This was empowering. I had teachers that instilled confidence, leadership, trust, and the desire to travel and see the world. I discovered new interests and passions.

I applied to, and got into, the University of Georgia – Go Dawgs! – and had an amazing four years in Athens, GA. I grew even more in college and became the woman I am today. I was on my own, doing my own thing. I already had the academic mindset, but in college I gained the social skills and the confidence I needed to succeed in life. During college, I learned how to be a leader, and the importance of being a mentor and a role model. I kept my eye on what I wanted with the goal of going to law school. The only reason I could attend college was because I had a scholarship that paid for my education. I graduated from the University of Georgia, Cum Laude with a double degree and a certificate. Graduating was bitter sweet. I enjoyed almost every day of my college career, and was not ready to leave Athens, but the time had come and my day had passed.

Coming out of college, I knew I could not immediately afford law school. I needed to work to save money, and I wanted to make sure law school was what I wanted to do. When I went to law school, I attended Mercer University. Law school was more about the theory of law, which seemed ridiculous to me. In my mind, I thought, "Who cares about theory? It's about the application." I did not enjoy law school as much as I had enjoyed every other educational experience. Law school was a necessary evil that I had to complete in order to practice law, and I got through it. When it came time for graduation, I didn't even attend my law school graduation. I was ready to be finished with law school and move on to the actual practice of law.

Becoming a wife and mother were both crucial moments in my life. I met my husband during my senior year in college. We dated in college for a brief period of time, but decided to remain friends. We lost touch for a few years but then ran into each other after college while living in Atlanta. I truly believe that everything happens for a reason. I had not seen him in a few

The Benefit of Using an Attorney-REALTOR®

years, but I immediately remembered him. We locked eyes, walked over to each other, and have been together ever since. We were married while I was in law school, and my marriage is a huge part of my identity. I can't imagine my life without my spouse. He is my support system and my rock; he's always there. Brett keeps me grounded and gives me a different perspective on things when I need it. Brett is my best friend and I am fortunate to have him in my life.

I'm also the mother of two daughters, which changes every aspect of my life. Being a mother adds a role to your life that you cannot fathom until you become a mother. You begin to see things differently and through your children's eyes. You want the world to be more innocent in order to protect your child, or at least preserve their virtue or naivety. As I age, I continue to ask myself, "Am I proud of what I am doing? Am I serving others? Would the girls be proud of what I am doing? Am I happy and do I enjoy what I am doing?" I think these are all important questions to ask oneself. Maybe it's old school to think of things in perspective of your sons and daughters, but I do.

I worked hard and try to stay focused on achieving happiness and success. I want my daughters to see that I can achieve great success and happiness, and so can they. As a parent, I want my children to feel secure in making their own decisions and having their own thoughts and opinions on certain topics. I want to instill in them the importance of standing up for yourself and what you believe in. Believing in something is important, and knowing why you believe in it is even more important.

Chapter 10

Legally Speaking

I decided at a young age that I wanted to be a professional, and be able to provide for myself and my family. Growing up, I watched a lot of shows like *Murder She Wrote, Colombo, Perry Mason, Scooby Doo* – and I loved *Nancy Drew* books. I decided I wanted to be a judge, and, over the years, that morphed into going to law school and becoming an attorney. It is funny to think back to my childhood, and the motivators behind what led to my career choice.

After college, I got a job at a mid-sized law firm, and started on the bottom rung. I took in every minute and absorbed everything. I was nervous when I started and I had no idea what to expect, but I did my best to embrace the moment and seize the opportunity. I started at the bottom, and, by the end of my law career, I was a partner at a large prestigious law firm. My first office at the firm was on the first floor in the middle of the building. It had no windows, and at one point I shared it with three to four other people. It's funny to think back to that office. I was sitting in that office on September 11, 2001, when the planes crashed into the Twin Towers – a moment I will never forget.

I worked at this firm for two years before going to law school, and clerked there for all three years of law school. I went from a law clerk to a paralegal, and then to an official law clerk while in law school. I sat in on depositions, attended hearings and mediations, and began writing briefs and delving into the daily jobs as an attorney. My knowledge and skills grew immensely during this time. In the first few months of working, it became clear that there were different types of attorneys, and every attorney practiced differently.

Some attorneys were efficient and knew how to do things from start to finish, while others did not know how to make copies, send out mail, or print documents. I learned so much from the secretaries, and some of the most valuable lessons I learned were from them. I saw firsthand that the secretaries were an integral part of what makes an attorney great. I saw attorneys who appreciated their secretaries and spoke kindly to them, and other attorneys who treated their secretaries poorly. It was surprising to me that they didn't realize what an asset they had with the secretaries. This was an important lesson for me. I became close to many of the secretaries and remain in touch with them to this day. The firm was very good to me and they were like family to me. I still value the knowledge and lessons they imparted on me.

During law school, I clerked for a judge, and had the opportunity to spend a significant amount of time with the judge. Spending time with the judge had a significant impact on me as a person and my law practice. I was fortunate enough to have significant one-on-one interaction with the judge. The judge was always open and honest with me and answered any and all questions. I had the opportunity to see many attorneys come in front of the judge, and the judge would give me pointers and tips on the best and worst practices. I learned a lot by watching the attorneys and seeing how they interacted with each other, their clients, the judge, and the courtroom staff.

The judge would tell me how he approached the law and cases. He had the power to determine a person's fate, which he did not take lightly. He made each decision thoughtfully and carefully, and always heard all of the evidence before making his decision. The judge treated each person in his courtroom with respect, regardless of who they were or what they had been charged with. He never forgot that each person was a person. I took that lesson with me in my legal career, and as a REALTOR®. Having this experience in law school was priceless to me in my life and career.

After law school, I started as an associate with a small to mid-size defense firm. I had an awesome experience at the firm. The firm was a great fit and I loved the partners and associates I worked with. I became very comfortable with my practice, and my confidence grew. As a defense attorney, I was responsible for billing my time, which meant that I had to keep track of what I did every six minutes. Yes, you read that correctly; every hour is broken up into six minute increments, and, in order to get paid, you had to keep track of your time. Lucky for me, I was an excellent biller. I got to the point where I felt I had achieved all I could on the defense side, so I decided to make the change to the plaintiff's practice.

I became a partner at a law firm and began representing individual people, and not corporations or large companies. There was a learning curve when I switched to the plaintiff's side. I was ready to help people and assist them with their cases. I believed that clients would be appreciative and thankful for my help and expertise; however, I quickly learned that some people are impossible to please, and, no matter what I did, how hard I worked, or how fantastic the outcome, some people would never be happy, and would always complain.

As a partner, I was in control of my cases and responsible for my law practice; however, I still answered to others because it was not my firm. As a partner, you are part of a larger practice, with a group of attorneys and a large support staff. There were things that had to be done as formalities that I had no control over. These things did not necessarily impact my practice directly, but affected the firm or the image of the firm.

I was responsible for myself and my staff, but there were things I would have changed or done differently if it were my firm. There were parts of the practice I liked, but many things that irritated me that I could not change. I was not free to make changes, or give my staff the day off if I was not working. I was always self-motivated and hard working. I had a desire to succeed and be on top of my law practice. I had never needed anyone breathing down my neck, or pressuring me to do things in my career that I didn't want to do. After five years working on the plaintiff's side, I decided that it was not for me. I was tired of the negativity, the long hours, the stress, and not being my own boss. I had achieved all I could have ever wanted or asked for in my law practice, but I still wasn't satisfied. I had to take an inward look and ask myself why. Why was I not satisfied? What was missing? What did I need to make me feel good and be happy with what I was doing?

I thought long and hard about these things before deciding what my next move would be. Over and over, I kept coming back to something I had been interested in since childhood – real estate. I did not think of it as real estate when I was young, but that was what it was, and it was something that always stayed with me. If I was going to get out of the practice of law, after spending so many years and so much money getting my law degree, I wanted to do something that I loved and that would make me happy. I wanted a career that would allow me to put my family first, which was never possible in my law practice; someone else came before me or my family.

I always insisted that the awesome team that worked for me put their families first, but I was in charge and had to ensure that the job was completed. The buck stopped with me. I sacrificed time with my family and loved ones in order to get the job done and meet the needs of my clients. If anyone on my team ever came to me needing time off for a family reason, I always said, "Family first," and told them to do what they needed to do. Why could I not tell myself the same thing? There were not enough hours in the day for me to provide the service I felt I had to provide to my clients, and also be the wife and mother I wanted to be.

Thank goodness I didn't lose any relationships or friendships during this time. I have amazing friends, but I allowed distance in my friendships, and I missed out on memories and moments due to a career that was not fulfilling my desires and needs. It was time for me to get control of my life. I had spent years of my life, and a significant amount of money to get my law degree, but it was not producing job satisfaction, or happiness in my personal life. It was time to move on, and find balance and success in all aspects of my life. Despite being on top of my career, I made the decision to leave the practice of law.

I was ready to create my own opportunities. Many people are afraid to act, or fear acting out of emotion, fearing it will result in poor choices, but I trust my inner voice. I had an entrepreneurial spirit since childhood, and I knew no one could ever match my work ethic. There was no reason for me not to be my own boss, because I would not allow myself to fail. *Kids Incorporated* did not fail when I was a child; in fact, it was successful, and I had the other neighborhood kids working for me. I went to law school for financial freedom and worked my way up to being a partner in a law firm under the guise that I would have freedom in my law practice, but none of that had panned out. It was time for me to take life by the horns and do what I wanted to do, and take advantage of opportunities when they came my way.

In my law practice, I told my clients, over and over, that none of us were guaranteed another breath, much less another day on this earth. No one can predict the future, or even what will happen in the next 12 hours, but, what is important, is to hold on to your loved ones, and not let any moment pass you by. Plenty of people say this, but don't live life that way. I was an example of that. It was time to take control and act. I quit the legal profession and decided that real estate was where I belonged. I am *for real* my own boss and the owner of my own company – Hope Ries, JD, REALTOR®, and author. I am creating opportunities and seizing the day for myself and my clients.

I am surrounded by positivity and a supportive, loving environment. I get to see my amazing husband and beautiful daughters, and spend more time with them then I ever did as an attorney. Every time the kids see a Berkshire Hathaway sign, they get excited. Both Brett and the kids have noticed a difference in me. I am walking taller and my smile is bigger. I have found my true calling. Going to law school, and practicing law, prepared me to be the best Attorney- REALTOR® that I can be. I offer my clients so much more than anyone else can offer them.

When I practiced law, I truly believed my clients were lucky to have me representing them. The same holds true in my real estate practice. My clients are lucky to have me and I am honored that they choose to work with me. I have not achieved the perfect balance in my life and I continue to strive for perfect balance. I continue to work towards being my best self, wife, and mother. As a REALTOR®, I can share my successes with my children and talk candidly about my career, which was not possible in my legal career.

I feel fulfilled in my real estate career because it is allowing me to serve others. My law degree is not going to waste, and I use it every day, but in a unique way. All of the lessons that I learned in the courtroom, and in the practice of law, have transitioned over into my real estate career. My legal background is a huge asset for my clients. I am miles ahead of other agents in so many aspects that it is laughable. I spent years honing and crafting my legal skills – my skills of thinking critically, reading and writing contracts, negotiating, and so many other talents unique to attorneys and litigators in particular. These talents serve me exceptionally well as a REALTOR®. Thinking back to law school, I would never have thought that I would be using these skills to help people purchase and sell homes; however, I cannot think of a better fit for my skills. The lessons I learned in my law practice and in the courtroom make me the perfect REALTOR®. Visit www.hoperiesattorneyrealtor.com for more information about me, Hope – or for information on listing your home, or purchasing a home.

About the Author

Hope Ries, JD, REALTOR®, was born in Marietta, Georgia. She is a licensed attorney and REALTOR®. She still lives in the community where she grew up, and remains involved in her community. She is happily married to her husband, Brett, and they have two beautiful daughters. Hope rose to the top of the legal profession with integrity. As a REALTOR®, Hope maintains the same level of professionalism and integrity. For more information about Hope, visit her website at www.hoperiesattorneyrealtor.com.

Made in the USA
Lexington, KY
05 December 2016